TWENTIETH-CENTURY ART FROM THE NELSON ALDRICH ROCKEFELLER COLLECTION

Distributed by New York Graphic Society Ltd., Greenwich, Connecticut

THE MUSEUM OF MODERN ART, NEW YORK

© 1969, The Museum of Modern Art

11 West 53 Street, New York, New York 10019

Library of Congress Catalogue Card Number 73-77512

Designed by Carl Laanes

Type set by Volk & Huxley, Inc., New York

Printed in the U.S.A. by

Lebanon Valley Offset Company, Inc., Cleona, Pennsylvania

Bound by Sendor Bindery, Inc., New York

frontispiece Picasso. Guitar. 1913. Pasted papers and charcoal, 24⅜ x 19⅛″

Contents

On behalf of the Trustees of The Museum of Modern Art, it is my privilege to thank the Honorable Nelson Aldrich Rockefeller for the extraordinarily generous loan of the works of art included in this exhibition. With great discrimination, Dorothy Miller has selected, from the approximately fifteen hundred works owned by the Governor, nearly a hundred paintings and as many sculptures and constructions, together with a number of watercolors and drawings. A sampling of his extensive collection of prints and illustrated books has been chosen by William S. Lieberman, who has also written a commentary on the collection.

In his Preface, Governor Rockefeller has provided insights into his lifelong impulse to acquire works of art, and into his public conscience with respect to ownership. As a preliminary to viewing this extraordinary collection, the reader may appreciate a further characterization of him as a connoisseur of art.

To a remarkable degree, he personifies this happy preoccupation, which in his case may be said to be hereditary. His grandfather, Nelson W. Aldrich, set him an impressive example. In public life, he served for many years as Senator from his native state of Rhode Island; he was also a collector of European art of the past, and the initiator of an important piece of legislation exempting it from tariffs. On the Rockefeller side, his grandfather and his father conveyed to their children a deep concern for educational philanthropies of all sorts. But (as Mr. Lieberman points out, page 11), it was his mother, Abby Aldrich Rockefeller, who stimulated an awareness of the arts of their own time in her children while they were still in their teens, and whose deep involvement with contemporary creativity led her to become one of the founders of The Museum of Modern Art.

Governor Rockefeller's present taste can surely be traced to his fortuitous first interests: European porcelain; American antique furniture and folk art; Southeast Asian artifacts, brought back from a world tour in 1930-31 (some of them not genuine, a fact which he gladly refers to as having taught him a useful lesson); twentieth-century masters, and the burgeoning contemporary production in this country; above all, perhaps, primitive art, beginning with the pre-Columbian, which he came to know early in the 1930s. In his enjoyment of primitive art, he has from the start been a true crusader and has done as much as any other American to assert its aesthetic worth, rescuing it from being the exclusive province of museums specializing in anthropology. To

this end, in 1957 he founded The Museum of Primitive Art. A selection from its collections (Art of Oceania, Africa, and the Americas) is being shown at The Metropolitan Museum of Art concurrently with this exhibition, and folk art from the Governor's collection is on view at The Museum of Primitive Art.

Certain equivalents between his successive early interests and the singularities of Governor Rockefeller's collecting to this day may be noted: an interest in the artist's direct expression, untheoretical and unaffected, and a liking for work making the dual appeal of emotional significance in relation to the overall culture of our day and age, as well as of aesthetic impact. His preference for simplicity may have turned him away somewhat from surrealism and the fantastic. Consciously or otherwise, he has maintained throughout his collection a predilection for sculpture; he himself might point out that this corresponds to the fact that modern America has been especially strong in three-dimensional art. To quote his words: "I am more drawn to the plastic, three-dimensional, than to pure line and color. I seriously considered being an architect when I was in college; perhaps my love for sculpture is related to my forgotten vocation."

Many important collectors of modern art have been high-principled and generous in sharing their possessions with their less privileged fellow art-lovers; few have been more so than Governor Rockefeller. On the occasion of its Twenty-fifth Anniversary, he gave to The Museum of Modern Art one of his greatest acquisitions, Rousseau's The Dream; and in 1963, in honor of Alfred H. Barr, Jr., he gave to the Museum Matisse's monumental Dance. Sixteen choice works from his collection, promised in 1958 as future gifts, are included in this exhibition.

Some collectors may have arrived at their generosity out of pride. In Governor Rockefeller's case, simple enjoyment and a sense of friendly obligation, more than any vain consideration, have prompted his policy. It was surely his desire to extend the opportunities for such enjoyment to as many others as possible that led him to initiate the New York State Council on the Arts, the first such body in the United States.

It may be of interest to try to examine his personality, his psychology, with regard to art, though this pertains to an inner infinitude of the mind, in essence impenetrable. No imperatives apply to it; nothing can be proved. What he represents and exercises is the modern mentality in art appreciation, very different from the old concern with antiquities, sequences of influences, attributions, and provenances. Brought up in a house resplendent with treasures—world-famous Chinese porcelains, the Unicorn Tapestries now at The Cloisters, Renaissance portraits—in his youth he knew little of the modern movement abroad, except that his mother believed in it, even in advance of her own enjoyment. For his part, he began at the beginning, with open experimental mind, learning both what older connoisseurs admired most and what gave him personal pleasure. At every point, his mother and he took it for granted that there were undiscovered areas out of sight, worthwhile productions not yet existent, not even conceived. Just as Mrs. Rockefeller consciously guided him in the direction of modern art, he influenced his son Michael, who as a boy tried his hand at painting and sculpture and went on to a creative aspect of anthropology (for which he gave his life), and who taught his father in turn. Today, Governor Rockefeller takes pride in the fact that his five-year-old son Nelson likes the neon-light constructions in his collection better than he does himself. This is a man not hampered by any generation gap in the arts, scarcely aware of one.

One of the jeopardies for an art collector is the commissioning of works of art for particular purposes. Here again we have the invisible, in the artist's mind; the collector cannot see into it. He has to dare and to gamble, manifesting an almost superstitious faith in the creative process. Again and again, Governor Rockefeller has risked it: with Matisse, Léger, Chagall, and Glarner.

Furthermore, in aesthetic matters as in politics and philanthropy, he has a warm democratic heart. Before the days of the WPA and government-sponsored art, The Museum of Modern Art asked a number of American artists to make designs for murals, for an exhibition. In one of them, the leftist artist William Gropper disobligingly made a satiric portrayal of J. P. Morgan. As chairman of the Advisory Committee in charge of the event, Nelson Rockefeller gravely put the matter before the great banker in person, who said, "Of course, exhibit it! Don't give it another thought." Governor Rockefeller has said recently that this, too, taught him a lesson of consequence: imperturbability and a sense of humor. Many a time, at the Museum, in Washington, and in Albany, he has responded to small crises of taste and discretion along this line and has backed Alfred Barr and René d'Harnoncourt in similar decisions.

His interest in the visual arts is not just a taste; it is an appetite and a nourishment. Mr. Barr has said: "His collection is large but so is his eager and chronic desire for more and more. Works of art give him a deep, almost therapeutic delight and refreshment such as other men find in music or alcohol. Nelson needs art more than any man I know of."

It gives him exercise, both mental and physical, rather than relaxation. When a new acquisition arrives, he insists on hanging it himself. The first three hours of his term of governorship he spent climbing on ladders to hang pictures, lugging pieces of sculpture around, seeking a harmonious way of fitting his Calders, Mirós, Lassaws, and Klines into the gingerbread Victorian decor of the Executive Mansion. The key to his experience of art, in both solitude and public service, is not pride nor the cult of culture; it is enjoyment.

All his friends and advisors have noted his intimacy with the art in his possession: a spiritual knowledge added to his visual and tactile familiarity. He carries a kind of catalogue of it in his head, as Balzac did the four hundred and sixty recurring characters in his *Comédie Humaine*. Amid his treasures, whether in Albany or Pocantico Hills or New York, whenever he can find time, given a listener or a group of listeners, he likes to serve as his own docent, and he does this admirably. It never embarrasses him to find others insensitive to the pleasure he takes himself. Wholeheartedly he will persuade you if he can, but with no objection to frustrations of his opinion, if it so happens.

All is empathy: the given work, a revelation of the true inner life of the man who produced it; the shared response to the given work (even a non-response, if it be respectful and frank), a form of humanism. For living art, in the frame of reference of its devotees, whom Nelson Rockefeller personifies, is the great unifier. It transcends political solutions, and the insolubles as well; it takes away snobbery and vertical distinctions of society and fortune; it connects the young and the old. In fact, the average enjoyer of art today is younger than the average creator of it; and they do connect, in a vast grid of vital interest, across the nation and around the world—an aesthetic nervous system. In this time of extreme acceleration of changes in taste, it is probably the younger generation's best access to their elders' experience and knowledge, the older generation's open window upon the potential of the men of the future.

I can't very well praise the present exhibition, because over the years I collected the various items that are in it; nor can I boast of the place where, to my great satisfaction, it is being exhibited, because of my close association and that of various members of my family with The Museum of Modern Art. My mother was one of the founders of the Museum; my elder brother's wife, my youngest brother, and I have all served as officers. So let me thank its several distinguished staff members who have kept me company and given me advice and assistance in the course of my collecting, particularly Alfred Barr. He is a man of universal knowledge about the arts of all time, with an extraordinary faith in modern art—as though it were a political principle or a religion. His scrupulous scholarship is joined with singular worldly wisdom and skillfulness, and he has made use of his reticence and stubbornness, along with other strengths of character, for the cause he had at heart.

René d'Harnoncourt, a man of traditional European subtlety and warmth, who truly loved whatever he admired, exchanging bonds of affection with all concerned, brought to the latter history of the Museum, when it had grown beyond the fondest dreams of its founders, a corresponding vigor and breadth of vision. It took his genius to draw the Trustees and other supporters, along with the staff, into intimacy and harmony, in what has surely been one of the greatest cultural undertakings of the free world.

Monroe Wheeler worked with my mother in the early days of the Museum and remains today one of its sturdy pillars. As an organizer of exhibitions, as the director in charge of the Museum's publications, as a man of impeccable taste and sensitivity, and as a friend and long-time associate, he too has been a wonderful companion in this adventure.

All these years, Dorothy Miller has been their close associate and most modest right hand, her latest undertaking having been the direction of this exhibition. Bill Lieberman, who joined the staff somewhat later as a very young man, represents a second generation, trained by his older colleagues and carrying on their high standards of excellence.

I seem to remember the shock and fresh pleasure and high hope generated in 1913 by the Armory Show, the first extensive showing in New York of avant-garde art—chiefly by Europeans, but with a good representation of Americans; but as I was then five years old, I must have in mind what I heard my mother and her friends say about it later. Another thing I remember is their lamenting the unreasonable lag between creation and appreciation. Some great artists died before their greatness was understood, and many of them had to toil away in poverty until they were past their prime before enjoying the rewards of their imagination and accomplishment. I think this was the true point of departure for those who made The Museum of Modern Art possible. And certainly it has succeeded in this respect.

Now I would like to say something about the relationship between museum and collector. From the start, Alfred and Dorothy set standards, as those of us who share their interests felt our way in these innovations of expression. They not only helped us to understand, but they gave us courage to make our own decisions. I like to think, and perhaps they would authorize me to say, that our unprofessional responsiveness gave an extra dimension to their responsible choices; and perhaps when Alfred wrote his now classic texts, he addressed them to us somewhat more directly than to the general museum public or his colleagues around the world. This, I believe, exemplifies a particular condition of art: it is a fraternal interest, non-egocentric in the artist, no matter how solitary and ahead of his time he may be; non-authoritarian for the museum director or the scholarly interpreter. They know and intend that the large public will catch up with them. Furthermore, the spirit of modern collecting is not miserly. Without the gifts and loans of thousands of collectors, there could have been no Museum of Modern Art.

I happen to know when artistic acquisitiveness first declared itself in my case. My mother had a sixth-century Chinese Bodhisattva; I loved it and wanted it, and she eventually agreed to leave it to me.

Many people have tried to see into the collector's mind. Cyril Connolly put it, perhaps too romantically, in a famous epigram: "Art is a religion; collecting is a form of prayer." Alfred Barr once attempted to subdivide the matter, mentioning speculation, prestige, competitiveness, and the wish to be envied; also *noblesse oblige,* beneficial to both the artist and the community at large.

In the last analysis—and probably Alfred would agree—it is a matter of love. One loves art, and wants to do something about it. Collecting and lending and bequeathing and, come to think of it, building museums to house one's bequests, are the things to be done.

I am often asked, and I ask myself, what art means to me. To answer this question as it deserves would entail a good deal of philosophy, even what is called semantics, and a self-examination as thorough as any question of conscience. But looking closely at art is a good game, sharpening one's wits and warming one's heart. It is the greatest recreation ever devised by the ingenious mind of man. It gives us relief from the pressures, frustrations, and compromises of everyday life. And without intellectual pretension or propaganda, I believe that it helps us to understand historic changes, fevers and ferments in the body politic, beneficial or otherwise—although spelling these things out in detail is apt to distort the artist's own purpose. In its nature, art is visionary; even if we fail to understand the artist's complex mentality, out of which so many disparate forms arise, the ambience of his free imagination stimulates in our minds dreamworlds and utopias of our own.

The most intense part of the spectator's experience of art is the absolute and unmixed attention that it commands. In the ordinary context of life, very few of us are capable of anything like this. It goes beyond pleasure, it is almost an ecstasy; and it is a discipline very conducive to strength in the other areas of our existence.

It is human nature to teach, and the desire to persuade those around us to share our pleasure is a part of it. In public life, I have encountered a good many men of consequence who are, or were, hostile to modernism in the arts, but even differences in this area are human and worthwhile. They give evidence of basic traits of character; they also throw light on the works of art in question, which one's own familiarity may not have illuminated. Even administrative activities having to do with the arts are instructive. I find that my early years in active and official capacity at the Museum have raised my sights and strengthened my hand in dealing with cultural affairs in Washington and Albany, planning for change, and broadening the availability of all the arts for all the people.

If this exhibition can bring to those who see it some fraction of the excitement and enjoyment that its contents have brought to me, then it will have served a great purpose.

de Chirico. The Song of Love. 1914. Oil, 28⅜ x 23½″

In May 1939, when he was not quite thirty-one, Nelson Aldrich Rockefeller became the second president of The Museum of Modern Art. In the course of a radio interview he answered several questions about himself, art, and the Museum:

"I'm interested in art that relates to life in our own day, that expresses the spirit of our time—art that isn't cloistered and set apart, art that includes the house and the motor car…as well as painting and sculpture….The true enjoyment of art is more than a vague and dutiful respect paid to the traditions of the past. At home, when we put a picture on the wall, I'm not so much interested in its historical value. I'm more interested in the pleasure it gives—the contribution it makes to the room and to the house. …What attracts me most about the art of our time is its vitality—the way it explores new possibilities and makes use of new materials….The Museum of Modern Art is trying to make the art of today useful and enjoyable to the public of today. Our contemporary arts need not wait fifty or a hundred years before they are widely appreciated….I think it's important that all forms of art reach the public—it's important that we know all about the flourishing arts of our own day."

In answer to a final question, "Do you enjoy having a share in this work?" he replied, "To be frank, I get a great kick out of it."

Two strengths nourish the lives of the family of John D. Rockefeller, Jr.: the ability to respect, and frequently to share, present-day concerns and enthusiasms; and the pursuit of broad visions, many of which seemed audacious at the time of their conception. Within the family, and across two (now three) generations, these strengths continue. They have produced extraordinary results, both public and private. One such flowering, the collection of modern art owned by Nelson Aldrich Rockefeller, is the subject of this exhibition.

Any discussion of his collection must consider two influences on Nelson Rockefeller: that of his mother, Abby Aldrich, and of the institution she helped to found, The Museum of Modern Art. Mrs. Rockefeller was in her fifties, and Nelson was at college, when she began to devote her major energies to collecting, studying, and exhibiting modern art. Although her husband supported and respected contemporary art, he frankly did not respond to her enthusiasm for it. In fact, he simply did not want to look at it. With some relief, he agreed that the children's former playroom on an upper floor of their house at 10 West 54th Street should be converted into a gallery. There Mrs. Rockefeller could place, in changing installations, her purchases of contemporary paintings, sculpture, drawings and prints; welcome friends and artists; and share her collection with the few who were interested in the art of their own time.

Nelson's own identification with modern art was immediate and positive. In 1927, he was a freshman at college and as usual spent Christmas vacation with his parents in New York. During the holiday recess, he visited the studio of Arthur B. Davies, and a Greenwich Village art gallery. On both occasions, his mother acted as cicerone. When he returned to Dartmouth, he wrote: "You don't know how much I enjoyed our two trips, to Mr. Davies and the visit to the Down Town Galleries. I feel as if I had been introduced to a new world of beauty, and for the first time I think I have really been able to appreciate and understand pictures, even though only a little bit. I hope to continue this when I am in New York and maybe do a tiny bit of collecting myself. I feel that was the outstanding event of my vacation."

His mother, of course, was highly pleased. She promptly replied: "If you start to cultivate your taste and eye so young, you ought to be very good at it by the time you can afford to collect. …Art is one of the great resources of my life. I believe that it not only enriches the spiritual life, but that it makes one more sane and sympathetic, more observant and understanding, regardless of whatever age it springs from, whatever subject it represents."

Later that year, she completed the gallery in the 54th Street house. Nelson was fascinated by what he saw there, and the dialogue with his mother about modern art continued before those paintings she had installed. But she had, in addition, another more civic project much on her mind. She wrote young Nelson that she had invited several critics to see "pictures that I have gotten together in my gallery….My mind is also full of ideas for a new Museum of Modern Art for New York. I have great hopes for it. Wouldn't it be splendid if it would be ready for you to be interested in when you get back to New York to live."

By the following November, The Museum of Modern Art had become a reality, A. Conger Goodyear its first president, and a young man of twenty-seven, Alfred H. Barr, Jr., who had been nominated by Professor Paul J. Sachs of Harvard University, its first director.

The next year, before Nelson Rockefeller was graduated from college, he was appointed to the Advisory Committee, a group of seventeen young people who were interested in modern art, as well as in the Museum's program. His mother had suggested that he be included "because he is extremely interested in modern art and he is the president of the Art Club at Dartmouth where he is a senior."

Subsequently, as chairman of the committee, Nelson Rockefeller was able to work closely with people of his own age, who shared his own interests; several among them were also to assume significant roles in the history of the Museum. In 1932, he became the first member of the Advisory Committee to be elected a Trustee of the Museum. Since then, he has twice been the Museum's president, and once the chairman of its board. His relationship with the Museum, in fact, has been a reciprocally creative one for forty years. This commitment has been a source of personal gratification to him, both as patron and private collector. The growth of his own collection has coincided closely with the growth of the Museum, which today continues to demand Nelson Rockefeller's judgment and directness, his enthusiasm and support.

Although Governor Rockefeller might acknowledge such classifications with surprise, his collection of twentieth-century art can be grouped into six categories, any one of which might provide material for a separate exhibition. His choice of European painting and sculpture of the first half of this century reveals three definite preferences: masterworks by the innovators of cubism and futurism; expressionism, defined in terms sufficiently broad and personal as to include Matisse and Modigliani; surrealism in sculpture, and its affinities in painting before and after the 1920s. Each of these three categories is supplemented as well by drawings and watercolors.

In American painting, a fourth category, Governor Rockefeller's preferences are more contemporary; for the most part, the examples were purchased soon after they were painted. These acquisitions demonstrate a particular commitment to the abstract expressionists who were painting in New York during the late 1940s and 1950s. His preferences in American sculpture, with two exceptions, reflect a similar emphasis on postwar work; but these choices should probably be included within a fifth and larger category: a selection of sculpture that (with a few omissions) offers an international survey of contemporary sculpture.

A last aspect of the collection has not grown significantly since Mr. Rockefeller was elected Governor of New York in November 1958. True enjoyment of prints and illustrated books needs the quiet and solitude of a contemplative life. This, perhaps the most intimate part of his collection, still remains a refuge and invites, indeed commands, repose. Only here does Governor Rockefeller reach back into the late nineteenth century and join the favorite enthusiasm of his mother. Mrs. Rockefeller, who had begun collecting in this field for the Museum as early as 1931, gave it 1600 prints in 1940 and continued to add others until her death in 1948. The Abby Aldrich Rockefeller Print Room, named in her honor, was opened the following year.

This exhibition can show only a small sampling of Governor Rockefeller's substantial holdings of modern prints and illustrated books, some of which are so rare that they may almost be considered unique.

The adventure of cubism determined much of the future course of twentieth-century art. Cubist painting lasted longer than the short-lived fauve movement, and its influence reached considerably further. The significance of cubism may be compared with that of another important development, abstract expressionism, which took place four decades later in the United States.

Governor Rockefeller owns several major works painted in France during cubism's heroic years, between 1907 and 1917. Taken together, they illustrate the development of cubism, while individually, they characterize the personal styles of the three dominant cubist masters—Braque, Picasso, and Gris. A consort to these works is Boccioni's famous futurist triptych, *States of Mind,* painted in Milan in 1911 and shown in Paris the next year.

Pablo Picasso's *Harvesters* of 1907, the earliest and least-known of these pictures, followed soon after his *Demoiselles d'Avignon.* Quickly painted, it is intense and brilliantly colored. The *Harvesters* (page 46) shows five haymakers at the left, a wain in the background, and at the right a tree and two cows. The scene recalls the landscape of the Andorra valley where Picasso had spent the previous summer. As articulated by color and form, the spatial relationships between the figures are unexpected, audacious, and perhaps unique in Picasso's art. Although the distortions and varying perspectives announce stylistic developments of the next ten years, the *Harvesters* cannot be considered as even a proto-cubist painting; it is one of Picasso's few fauve essays.

In Paris in the early months of 1908 and 1909, Picasso painted two versions of a seated woman with a mandolin, one nude, the other dressed. During the winter of 1910, he twice repeated the same theme: in *Girl with a Mandolin* (page 47) and in an oval composition, also included in this exhibition.

The monochromatic *Girl with a Mandolin* is essential to a review of cubism—indeed, to any exposition of twentieth-century art. It is an explicit summary of earlier analytic cubism. Several decades later, Picasso identified the woman as Fanny Tellier, and some critics have inferred therefore that he painted directly from the model. This, however, is irrelevant. The sitter's identity is far more generalized than in any of his cubist likenesses of male friends. The picture is a simple application of cubist principles to a convention of figure-painting that had been established in France in the mid-nineteenth century by Corot, a painter whom Braque also deeply admired.

Girl with a Mandolin is one of Picasso's clearest solutions to a formal problem: the human body as a subject for cubist analysis. In *Girl with a Mandolin,* two rounded forms—the prominent right breast, and the body of the mandolin—reflect the plastic and sculptural concerns of analytic cubism. The musical instrument is modeled with greater realism than the human anatomy, whose forms are for the most part flattened and squared. In addition to the breast and mandolin, two smaller areas, the eye and the cursive chignon (the only features that might identify a specific model) relieve the system of straight planes that reduces the figure to geometric shapes and displaces, blocks, and composes a generally ordered structure.

It is tempting to speculate how a futurist painter might have viewed the same subject. Picasso's woman, however, is in repose. Her head inclines gently, and her playing is without movement. The background, against which the body seems suspended, is more obscure. A stretched accordion of solid rectangles, it is not immediately intelligible.

At this time, the friendship between Braque and Picasso was at its most intimate, and for a few months their personal styles were so similar as to seem interchangeable. Braque painted the same subject in the same pose at least twice; and many years later, Alfred Barr wrote Nelson Rockefeller that he had discovered a drawing by Braque that directly copies Picasso's *Girl with a Mandolin.*

Six still lifes in the Rockefeller collection illustrate the further evolution of cubism. Two are small, compact paintings by Picasso. Approximately the same size, they invite comparison. In the earlier, *Still Life: Le Torero,* painted at Céret in the summer of 1911 (page 48), the bottle of rum, carafe, and glasses are transformed into a cascade of straight lines and planes. The objects themselves have all but disappeared, and there is no distinction between background and foreground—or, as Nelson Rockefeller says, "subject matter drops into the background." The forms are completely fragmented. Their decomposition is starkly relieved by the placement of the black letters, "Le T..." and "Tau[reau]." But the painting has nothing to do with bulls or bullfighters. The painted imitation of printed letters is a formal, not contextual, element of the composition, and a prelude to collage. The picture, which with the exception of the letters shows Picasso at his most abstract and cubism at its most extreme, was formerly owned by the artist's close friend, the French poet Paul Eluard.

In Picasso's later *Still Life: "Job,"* 1916 (page 48), the monochromes of analytic cubism have been replaced by a brighter, wider range of colors. On a fringed tablecloth sit a bowl of grapes, a bottle of rum, and a pack of cigarettes, whose brand name lends the painting its title. Although the arrangement of the objects is completely free, their forms are more clearly defined, and thus more readable than in *Le Torero.* In contrast to the painted letters in that picture, the letters of *"Job"* identify an object, the pack of cigarettes. The textures of the painting's surface, also, are more varied; actual grains of sand and ash have been mixed with the paint. A pointillist technique, introduced into cubism two years previously, further enlivens several passages.

"Job," which may be regarded as a collage made without paper or paste, could have been painted only after Picasso's experience of that medium. It anticipates a direction of synthetic cubism, which became increasingly decorative and, in Governor Rockefeller's collection, culminates with Picasso's sumptuous *Pitcher and Bowl of Fruit* of 1931 (page 62).

Although cubism was considered a revolutionary style at the time it was developed, actually it evolved from a study of Cézanne, and put to new uses many of his concepts. The introduction of collage was far more radical, for here disparate objects and materials, usually of paper, were affixed to the picture's surface. Since these elements were used to describe things rather than people or landscapes, cubist collages are almost always still lifes. Three examples in the Rockefeller collection are alike in their iconography: the references to music so favored by Braque, Picasso, and Gris. Although these works demonstrate the personal techniques of the respective artists as

makers of collage, more important is the fact that they share a common aesthetic. In these constructions, *trompe l'oeil*—in the past a virtuoso variation of still-life painting—is achieved by the use of actual materials rather than by illusionistic imitation.

Picasso's *Guitar* of 1913 (frontispiece), a painterly collage, is completely constructed of a variety of papers, including, somewhat exceptionally, a clipping from a Spanish newspaper. Braque's *Clarinet,* also of 1913 (page 49), appears less cluttered and more classic. It is, without a doubt, the most elegant of all his collages. It accords perfectly with Guillaume Apollinaire's description in *The Cubist Painters,* published in the same year: "Peaceful appearances in plastic generalization are joined once more in a temperate zone by the art of Georges Braque."

Although elements of Braque's *Clarinet* are bound to canvas, essentially it is a drawing in black, brown, and charcoal, with large areas of white untouched. The paraphernalia of the still life are arranged within an oval, a shape particularly favored by the cubists. Sometimes the canvas is mounted on an oval stretcher; sometimes, as here, the oval floats within a rectangle. The *Clarinet,* with its order, balance, and symmetry, is one of Governor Rockefeller's favorite pictures and was also a favorite of his third son, Michael.

Juan Gris was the most representational, and perhaps the most lucid, of the cubist painters. In his own words, he had "witnessed the birth of cubism, adopted it shortly afterwards and exhibited for the first time at the Salon des Indépendants in 1912." In the summer of 1914, when he was twenty-seven, Gris fled wartime Paris. For personal reasons, he could not return to Spain, and he settled instead near the border at Collioure, a small fishing village on the Mediterranean. When he returned to Paris in November, he brought with him six paintings, and three collages—one of which is the *Guitar, Bottle, and Glass* (page 51) in the Rockefeller collection. Like Braque's *Clarinet,* Gris's *Guitar, Bottle, and Glass* is an oval still life contained within a rectangle, this time a vertical one. Its intermingled combinations of pasted papers, paint, and drawing are exquisitely resolved and are very characteristic of Gris. The checkered pattern is also typical of his art. The contrasts of gray and black, green and brown, are warm and subdued. The multiple views of the glass illustrate perfectly the cubists' preoccupation with the presentation of several aspects of the same object at the same time. The guitar also serves as table, with a leg breaking through the oval.

Gris spent most of 1917 in Paris. Although by this time the cubists had abandoned collage, his austere and soaring *Sideboard* (page 55) owes much to its inventions. Cubism was never wholly abstract, and Gris himself best described his aims in a letter to his friend, the dealer Daniel-Henry Kahnweiler:

"I would like to continue the tradition of painting with plastic means while bringing to it a new aesthetic based on the intellect. I think one can quite well take over Chardin's means without taking over either the appearance of his pictures or his conception of reality. Those who believe in abstract painting seem to me like weavers who think they can produce a material with threads running in one direction only and nothing to hold them together. When you have no plastic intention how can you control and make sense of your representational liberties? And when you are not concerned with reality how can you control and make sense of your plastic liberties?...I have also managed to rid my painting of a too brutal and descriptive reality. It has, so to speak, become more poetic. I hope that ultimately I shall be able to express very precisely, and by means of pure intellectual elements, an imaginary reality. This really amounts to a sort of painting which is inaccurate but precise, just the opposite of bad painting which is accurate but not precise."

Three other paintings in Governor Rockefeller's collection also belong to these heroic years and are stylistically allied to cubism; indeed, they derive from it. The content of these paintings by Umberto Boccioni, however, is quite different; it evokes "states of mind," and is a subjective illustration of modern man's preoccupation with his own emotions.

With the exception of the landscapes that they painted during the summers, Braque, Picasso, and Gris limited their subject matter to objects and people of the café and the studio—reflecting a bohemian, somewhat private life. The futurists, on the other hand, and Boccioni in particular, adapted the language of cubism to different purposes. Unlike the cubists, the futurists considered themselves against tradition. They were concerned with two problems: one formal—the visual description of movement; the other social—man's identity within a new and mechanized world of his own making. Their large compositions, with figures placed against the architectural setting of the modern city, throb with the pulse of metropolitan life.

Boccioni's first significant painting, *The City Rises,* was begun in 1910, the year in which he joined with four other painters in signing the Technical Manifesto of Futurist Painting. Late in 1911, after his return from Paris, where he experienced his first direct contact with cubism, he painted *States of Mind* (pages 52–53). The formal and stylistic differences between each of the panels that compose Boccioni's triptych are not subtle. The three paintings are unified by flat and consistent rhythms, which move tumultuously, diagonally or vertically, across the surface of each canvas.

The triptych is a dramatic narrative. Its interrelated subjects involve transportation, a machine, and people—those who travel by train, their method of departure, and the others who remain behind. The smoking locomotive in *The Farewells* divides a swelling crowd. The arabic numerals stenciled on the cab derive, of course, from cubism; but their use here is not completely formal, since, like the black roman numerals "I" and "III" painted at the right and left of the central panel, *Those Who Go,* to designate first- and third-class carriages, they serve to indicate parts of the train. In *Those Who Stay,* visitors retreat across the station's platform. Their movement is arrested, dragging, and sad, spaced within the vertical accents that grid the picture. In *Those Who Go,* the train's speed is rendered by diagonal and rounded thrusts, which oscillate and unite the staring faces of the passengers with the landscape that unfolds before them.

Braque's vertical *Table,* 1930 (page 59), and Picasso's horizontal *Pitcher and Bowl of Fruit,* 1931 (page 62), lie beyond cubism's historic confines. Both are large paintings, decorative in conception. Their perspectives remain flattened, as in cubism, but the overall patterns of these still lifes are less rigorous and more ornate. The Braque belongs to a series of paintings of this kind of round-topped table *(guéridon)* that continues into the 1930s. The table, bowl of fruit, mandolin, and sheets of music recall the iconography of cubism, as do the staccato, pointillist brush strokes (which also occur in the Picasso). As in the Picasso, the forms are more flowing, and the colors less inhibited than in earlier cubist works. The textured grains that enrich the surface of the painting deliberately reduce the sheen of the oil paint.

There are fewer kinds of objects in Picasso's still life, but its composition is more intricate. Although the silhouettes of the forms are isolated and heavily outlined, their spatial relationships are never clarified. The brilliant colors shine through the heavy borders of the shapes with the luminosity of stained glass within its leading. Beneath the dark outlines, ribbons of lighter colors cross the surface of the painting in straight lines and sweeping curves.

Fernand Léger, who was influenced by cubism earlier than Gris, stands somewhat apart from the two Spaniards or his fellow Frenchman, Braque. His paintings are direct and rarely speak with the lyric qualities that characterize cubism. His forms are seldom transparent, as in cubist painting; they are volumes, cylindrical and architectonic. Léger does not attempt to examine different aspects of an object; rather, he repeats its shape. His painting seems most germane to cubism between 1910 and 1914; in 1912, he was also influenced by futurism.

The Great War disbanded the unity of the cubist painters. Léger was drafted into the French Army in 1914, serving in the engineering corps, and was wounded and discharged three years later. His observation of war machines helped him to develop a personal style that he had begun to conceive as early as 1910. It is somehow appropriate that Léger is represented in this exhibition by a painting celebrating the end of the war in 1918. The small, brilliantly colored *Armistice* (page 56), with its almost enameled surface, parades a profusion of flags (one American) seen from a window. This is not a glorification of the modern metropolis; the little painting is intimate and, for Léger, unexpectedly lively.

Like so many works in Governor Rockefeller's collection, a second painting by Léger, *Woman with a Book* of 1923 (page

57), seems difficult rather than pretty. To Léger, who was strongly influenced by the machine aesthetics of Le Corbusier and Amédée Ozenfant, there is no distinction between man, animal, and object: "One may consider the human figure not for its sentimental value but only for its plastic value. That is why in the evolution of my work since 1905 until now the human figure has remained purposely inexpressive." The woman stands like a hieratic statue, confronting the modern world. This statue can neither move nor breathe; its frontality is aggressive and unrelieved. The neck rises like a column, the arms are rigged to the body, the hair is burnished metal. The figure is sexless, the face plain, symmetric, immobile, and devoid of all expression. The beautiful pattern of the composition owes as much to the impedimenta of book and flowers as it does to the woman herself.

Léger's preoccupation with mechanical forms was expressed only two-dimensionally, on the surface of his paintings or in his film, *Ballet Mécanique,* made in the year following the *Woman with a Book.* The sculptor Raymond Duchamp-Villon, however, composed forms in three dimensions, which interact as do the elements of a collage, to produce a construction.

In the First World War, Duchamp-Villon was enlisted with the Cuirassiers (the cavalry regiment glorified in two paintings by another cubist, Roger de La Fresnaye); and, like Léger, he saw the terrible new machines made by man. Duchamp-Villon was confounded by the anachronism of the horse as a means of transportation. He became so obsessed with this paradox that, in 1914, he decided actually to transform the horse into a machine—a noble one. He sought to reduce, reveal, and combine in sculpture the anatomy, spirit, and movement of the animal. Working in plaster, he made seven small statues, and as the series progressed, the figure of the horse became increasingly abstract. After his death in 1918, the last of these versions was enlarged twice—first, in 1930–31, to forty inches high, and later, in 1966, to almost five feet high. It is shown here (page 54) at its most dramatic, in the larger version—often known as *Le Cheval majeur.* This beast is itself a hero, an equestrian monument without a rider.

To appreciate and understand the simultaneous and different aspects of *The Horse,* the spectator should walk around the sculpture, or the piece itself should turn. Its dynamic spiral recalls Boccioni's sculptured still life, *Development of a Bottle in Space,* and indeed Duchamp-Villon frequently seems closer to futurism than to cubism. Both Duchamp-Villon and Brancusi had wished to see final versions of certain of their works in stainless steel, but unfortunately the posthumous casts of Duchamp-Villon's horse were all done in bronze.

Constantin Brancusi's *Bird in Space* (page 61) exists in several versions. That in the Rockefeller collection measures more than six feet high and is one of the tallest in the series that Brancusi began in 1923. It was carved with extraordinary craft from a single block of white marble. The balanced taper of the solid

Lipchitz. Song of the Vowels. 1931–32

rounded form soars with simple grace and strength. Brancusi's elegant monolith contrasts with the open, somehow more vulnerable, interacting parts of Duchamp-Villon's horse.

Brancusi was not a cubist, and his aesthetic is quite different in its purpose, origins, and development from that of Duchamp-Villon. He sought the embodiment of spirit, not character; the visualization of motion, not movement. Brancusi distills meaning; he was never concerned with the specific. Unlike the cubists, he did not analyze form into its component parts. Instead, he refined his subjects—for example, the bird—into universal generalizations.

Two other sculptors, Jacques Lipchitz and Alexander Archipenko, who were working in Paris at about the same time, did translate the canons of cubism into three dimensions. Lipchitz's first friends in Paris were the Mexican painter Diego Rivera, who was scorned by the founding cubists, and the Italian Amedeo Modigliani, who at that time was studying sculpture, briefly, with Brancusi. Among the cubists, Gris is closest to Lipchitz. In this exhibition, Lipchitz is represented by his *Seated Man with Guitar,* 1922 (page 58), carved from granite. It is one of the most successful in a series of cubist interpretations of guitar players begun by Lipchitz in 1914. It was subsequently cast in bronze in an edition of seven. The major work by Lipchitz in the Governor's collection is one of the artist's greatest monuments, the *Song of the Vowels* of 1931–32 (page 15), now permanently installed at Pocantico Hills and not available for this exhibition. It was shown in Lipchitz's retrospective exhibition at The Museum of Modern Art in 1954.

An exhibition of cubist sculpture limited to the two decades after 1909 might demonstrate the significance of Archipenko. It would be revealing, and his stature would increase, if his work could be viewed in context with earlier works by Picasso, Duchamp-Villon, and Lipchitz, and contrasted with sculpture by Henri Laurens and Ossip Zadkine. Like the Lipchitz, Archipenko's *Standing Woman,* 1923 (page 58), is directly carved and is small in size. It repeats one of his earlier plaster figures and coincides in time with the first wood carvings by Henry Moore. The medium, mahogany, is unusual in Archipenko's work.

The ramifications of cubism and the influence of collage were not limited to France. In the Netherlands, Piet Mondrian and his friends developed a geometric and rectangular style, derived from cubism; but unlike cubism, it resulted in complete abstraction. Mondrian's *Large Composition A* (page 60), almost exactly square, pushes the liberties of cubism to an extreme and completely disengages the artist from any reference to the object.

In France, the cubists ceased to make collages after 1917. In Germany, however, several of the dadaists adopted collage and, indeed, transformed it, often with wit. Kurt Schwitters, whose approach to the medium was highly individual, continued to compose collages throughout his career. His constructions are abstract and vary considerably in size; they rarely conceal the shapes and origins of the pasted papers that he collected from the debris of daily life to use in them. Governor Rockefeller owns a bouquet of small collages by Schwitters ranging in date from 1921 to 1946; all are included in this exhibition (page 78).

The flowing freedom of art nouveau, the first truly international modern style, was a major source for the conflagration of expressionism, which spread through Europe shortly after 1900. If one accepts a broad definition, expressionism is a form of mannerism. The visual articulation of emotion and the inner self, and the subjective interpretation of observed form, need not necessarily be keyed to trauma. The employment of autonomous color and stylistic distortion can be decorative, as well as dramatic. When the use of these devices is pushed to an extreme, however, the result may seem pathological.

Within the span of a relatively few years, expressionist styles developed almost simultaneously in France with the fauves ("wild beasts"), in Germany with the group known as Die Brücke ("The Bridge"), and with two Russian contemporaries, Alexey Jawlensky and Wassily Kandinsky. Though their styles evolved independently, there were personal contacts among many of these artists and numerous crosscurrents of influence.

In contrast to the brotherhood of Die Brücke, founded in Dresden in 1905, the fauves were never a cohesive group. Neither were they obsessed by modern man's discovery of his own psyche, the exploration of which so insistently haunted the expressionists in Germany. Fauve painting is structured on form rather than on content; its patterns are bold and bright. The fauve painters were particularly attracted to views of rivers and ports, always with reference to the safe, adjacent land. In 1905, Henri Matisse and his family began to summer in Collioure, the small fishing village near the Spanish border in which Gris was to spend the summer of 1914 (see above). It was at Collioure that Matisse and André Derain painted the first fauve pictures. Matisse's landscape of the harbor of Collioure in Governor Rockefeller's collection (page 38) is, however, somewhat later. It dates from 1911 and anticipates, curiously, Pierre Bonnard's paintings of another French Mediterranean port, Cannes.

In *Collioure,* Matisse observes the scene almost as if it were a stage set viewed from the balcony of a theater. Looking down and through a proscenium of trees painted dark blue, one sees the small peninsula, which protects the waters of the bay. The overall design of the painting is not characteristically fauve, for the contrast between the silhouette of the foreground and the landscape below is calculated and disciplined. The colors and shapes, however, are painted with the utmost freedom.

Matisse was in his mid-thirties before his art found its direction. He was the dominant personality of the fauves, whose loose association was of short duration. Like most of his companions, he abandoned the wild freedom of the fauve palette for more controlled but generally joyous color.

The fauves first exhibited publicly in Paris in the autumn of 1905. Shortly thereafter an American family, the Steins, consisting of Gertrude, her brothers Leo and Michael, and Michael's wife Sarah, became Matisse's first important patrons. (They were also important early patrons of Picasso; his sheet of drawings, *Study for "The Actor" with Profiles of Fernande,* 1904–05, owned by Governor Rockefeller, was formerly in the collection of Gertrude Stein.) Other American collectors also became interested in Matisse's art—Dr. Claribel and Miss Etta Cone of Baltimore among them. Only one other American family was to have as long an involvement with Matisse: the Rockefellers. The relationship, which began in 1930, lasted for twenty-five years, and in fact Matisse's last work was a stained-glass window commemorating Abby Aldrich Rockefeller. That work, and Matisse's connections with the Rockefeller family, will be discussed below. Meanwhile, with reference to Matisse's earlier work, it should be noted that the *Reclining Nude* of 1907 in Governor Rockefeller's collection (page 40) is a translation into bronze of one of Matisse's major fauve paintings: the imposing *Blue Nude* of the same year, which was first owned by Leo Stein, later by the Cone sisters, and is now in the Cone Collection at the Baltimore Museum of Art. The statue of the *Reclining Nude* was in turn incorporated by Matisse into later paintings; and subsequently, in 1929, its subject and pose were again repeated in one of his sculptures. It is also related to drawings and prints by Matisse. Similarly, a second Matisse bronze owned by Governor Rockefeller, the *Seated Nude* of 1925 (page 40), relates intimately to another smaller bronze by Matisse, as well as to a series of lithographs of odalisques—the last of which is included in this exhibition (page 21).

Besides the Steins and the Cones, one of the most important of Matisse's early patrons was a Russian businessman, Sergei I. Shchukin, who in the decade preceding the First World War was the greatest collector of modern French painting in the world. Early in 1909, he commissioned from Matisse two murals, *Dance* and *Music,* for the stair landing of his house in Moscow. Final versions of these were completed by Matisse in 1910 and are now in The Hermitage in Leningrad. The first version of the *Dance* (page 23), painted early in 1909, lay for years rolled up in Matisse's studio before being sold in 1936 to Walter P. Chrysler, Jr. In 1963, it was bought by Governor Rockefeller, who generously presented this great and historic masterpiece of the modern movement to The Museum of Modern Art in honor of Alfred Barr, his friend for over three decades. *Dance* repeats the motif of the ring of dancers to be seen in the background of Matisse's large canvas, *Joy of Life,* which was bought in 1906 by Leo and Gertrude Stein and is today in the Barnes Foundation at Merion, Pennsylvania. The theme had been inspired by the wild round dances of Catalan fishermen, which it is said Matisse had watched on the beach of Collioure in the summer of 1905 and had once been inspired to join.

Picasso. Study for "The Actor" with Profiles of Fernande. 1904–05

Another of Matisse's earlier paintings owned by Governor Rockefeller is the *Italian Woman* of 1915 (page 39), which had previously belonged to the great New York collector of modern art, John Quinn. Like Picasso's *Girl with a Mandolin,* the *Italian Woman* is one of several masterpieces in a gallery of modern portraits. Governor Rockefeller, however, has little interest in the identity of the sitter, an Italian model named Lorette, but says tersely: "It's simple and it's strong." The painting, with its warm colors and bold ellipse, owes much to Matisse's observation of cubism. It is one of a series of monumental single figures that he painted between 1913 and 1917.

In his paintings of the nude and his use of the female figure as decoration, Modigliani is closer to Matisse than any other artist painting in Paris in the years around the First World War. His career was brief; he died at the age of thirty-six. As has been said, he studied sculpture with Brancusi for a short time and executed a few works in that medium, but he is best known as a painter. His range of subjects is much more limited than Matisse's; with the exception of three landscapes, Modigliani's paintings are confined to likenesses of his friends, acquaintances, and casual pickups. His nudes glorify the female form, which he adored. Like Matisse, he always worked from the model. The Rockefeller collection brings together in fascinating association the two bronze nudes by Matisse (page 40) and Modigliani's *The Dreamer* of 1918 (page 41), which is similar to them in pose.

Modigliani's reclining nudes offer the only horizontal images in his art. Silhouetted against a dark background almost immediately behind her, the elongated torso of *The Dreamer* stretches diagonally across the picture plane. The model drapes her arms behind her head in a gesture reminiscent of a Venus by Giorgione, or an odalisque by Ingres (or Matisse). The contours of her body and the features of her face are soft, and more sculpturally rounded than in Modigliani's other likenesses of women. The model's expression is somewhat wistful, her pose pliant and supine. Modigliani brings felicitously to a close a mannerist tradition of Italianate painting in France that goes back to the School of Fontainebleau in the sixteenth century.

The passionate tragedy of his life has cast Modigliani, like Vincent van Gogh, as a romantic hero. His actual achievement lies somewhat outside the mainstream of twentieth-century art; but, in his series of some twenty nudes, what glorious paintings he made!

Two Russian contemporaries of the fauves, Jawlensky and Kandinsky, evolved a style similar to theirs. Their early paintings, however, seem flatter than those of the fauves and seldom attempt illusionistic perspective. Although their colors appear even more vivid, perhaps because of the contrasting use of black, they are in fact more naturalistic. The opaque tonality of these colors, as well as the method of application, owes some inspiration to the folk arts of Russia and Bavaria.

It is difficult to believe that Jawlensky painted the haunting *Cottage in the Woods* as early as 1903, although it is so marked on its reverse. The placement of the tree and its shadow is daring, and the panel bristles with divisionist color.

In 1907, Jawlensky met Matisse in Paris, and in the same year renewed his acquaintance with Kandinsky in Munich. For a short while, the friendship of the two Russians became as close and intense as that of Braque and Picasso in Paris a few years later. In 1908 and 1909, they summered with their mistresses in Murnau, a village in Southern Bavaria. It was there that Kandinsky painted *Autumn Landscape, Murnau,* 1908 (page 42).

The forms in this painting, like those in Jawlensky's *Spanish Girl,* 1912 (page 43), are heavily outlined in black. The decorative use of discordant color, however, allies the two Russians with the fauves rather than with the German expressionists. In the Jawlensky, the model's head characteristically fills the rectangle of the picture. The vulgarity of her coarse, heavily made-up features is relieved by the headdress, whose haloed contour softens the flat angularity of her face. *Spanish Girl* is painted in oil on paper, a medium favored for several years by Jawlensky and Kandinsky. Its use may explain why some of their pictures of this period so often lack transparency and depth of color.

Kees van Dongen, the one member of the fauves who was not French by birth, was the stylistic link between the fauves and the Brücke brotherhood in Dresden. In 1908, they invited van Dongen to become a member of their group, and he exhibited a number of prints and drawings with them in Germany. In the same year, he held his second one-man show in Paris. His *Woman in a Large Hat* (page 44) was also painted in that year. Its technique remains fauve, but its style is as mundane as the subject is elegant, foreshadowing the later direction of his art.

Georges Rouault was for a time associated with the fauves and continued to a later date the tradition of expressionist painting in France. *The Judge,* painted by Rouault in 1930, was a gift to Nelson Rockefeller from his mother. He also owns Rouault's great series of etchings, the *Miserere.* This copy, which he bought directly from the artist the year after its publication in final form, contains a poem especially composed for him by Rouault. At the same time he acquired several trial proofs, some colored, of Rouault's illustrations for Baudelaire's *Les Fleurs du mal.*

It is impossible not to wonder whether Governor Rockefeller did not subconsciously recall *The Judge* when, in 1949, he purchased Max Beckmann's *Woman with a Parrot* (page 90). The paintings have in common a suggestion of allegory, the profile view, the contours of the shoulders and arms, the heavy outlines, and even a rectangle in the background.

Beckmann was not directly allied with German expressionism, but his *Woman with a Parrot,* a relatively late work, is the only painting in Governor Rockefeller's collection that is in any way related to that tradition. It was painted in Amsterdam in 1946, a year after the liberation of the Netherlands (where Beckmann had settled after the Nazis, in 1936, declared his art "degenerate"), and a year before he and his wife emigrated to the United States. This picture of a woman seated beside a piano is as mannered as Modigliani's *Dreamer,* and as handsome.

Although Governor Rockefeller owns no works by the German expressionists active in the first quarter of the twentieth century, he does own a number of works in sculpture by their contemporaries: Ernst Barlach, Georg Kolbe, Gerhard Marcks, and Wilhelm Lehmbruck. Of his two cast-stone pieces by Lehmbruck, the small *Dancer* of 1913–14 (page 45) was purchased in 1939. The elegant *Torso* of 1910 (page 45) he received in 1950 as a gift from his friend Wallace Harrison, the architect of Rockefeller Center.

Certainly the greatest expressionist painter of the twentieth century is Picasso. His most expressionist work in the collection is a painting of the mid-1930s. During 1934, he had painted several vertical compositions of two girls seated at a table, their eyes downcast as they read, write, or draw. In February 1935, he resumed the theme in two large horizontal paintings, which are quite similar in composition: each has a mirror at the left, a table with a bouquet of flowers, and two girls seated on the floor—one asleep, the other drawing.

Of the two paintings, Governor Rockefeller's is the larger. To a Picasso enthusiast, the *Interior with a Girl Drawing* (page 63) is particularly fascinating. The sinuous and heavily outlined curves evident in the related paintings of the previous year are here modified by angular accents, particularly in the furniture and the figure at the right. Underneath the picture lies another one, which Picasso had photographed and elaborately annotated in a drawing before painting over it. This first version was even more angular, and it differs in several other respects: the table was smaller, the background uncurtained, the two women farther apart, and the one at the right lacking the garland of flowers which, in the final version, crowns her head.

In 1930, a far more classic painting by Picasso, *Portrait of Madame Picasso,* 1923, was awarded First Prize at the 29th Carnegie International Exhibition in Pittsburgh. One member of the three-man jury was Matisse, who three years before had won the corresponding award, and who now had the opportunity to make a kind of *grand geste* by joining the two American jurors in giving the prize to his great peer. Before returning to France, he visited the two most important Matisse collections in the United States, that of the Barnes Foundation in Merion, Pennsylvania, and of Miss Etta Cone in Baltimore, and then came to New York, which he had passed through briefly earlier in the year en route to Tahiti.

Among the private collectors in New York who were eager to meet him was Mrs. Rockefeller. Nelson Rockefeller was at that time in the Dutch East Indies (where he acquired his first primitive object, a knife-handle from Sumatra); but his mother wrote

above Rouault. The Judge. 1930
below Jawlensky. Cottage in the Woods. 1903

to his brother, Laurance, then at Princeton, inviting him to a dinner she was giving for Matisse on December 18th, and promising her son that if he could come, "I will try to get another girl. You can suggest anyone you like so long as she is good-looking...I am told that Matisse very much likes pretty girls." Among the guests was Frank Crowninshield, a founding Trustee of the Museum. He has described the evening (including the young ladies, who were not only pretty, but like many American beauties, also tall):

"After the coffee, Monsieur Matisse turned to Mr. Rockefeller and began, half seriously, to plead his cause; to explain that the men who had created the incredibly beautiful green, yellow, red, and black porcelains that were all about us, were really in pursuit of exactly the same aesthetic goals as those to which Matisse had personally dedicated himself. He tried, too, to convince him that Braque, Juan Gris, and Picasso had merely followed the decorative designs and emotive experiences of the Persians who had woven what Matisse called Mr. Rockefeller's 'modern' (though seventeenth-century) Polonaise rugs; that, in short, there was no such thing as modern art, or ancient art, or art of the Middle Ages; that the deadest art imaginable was that of the hack painters who now flourish in so many of our academies of art.

"But the philanthropist, who had listened very politely, regretted, quite as politely, and in the most polished French, that he must still appear adamant. Then, with an engaging burst of confidence, he added that Mr. Matisse must not altogether despair because though he might still seem to be stone, he suspected that Mrs. Rockefeller, thanks to her very special gifts of persuasion, would eventually wear him down to the consistency of jelly." (She did not.)

Less than a year later, The Museum of Modern Art gave its first large one-man show of a European artist to Matisse. Organized by Alfred Barr, it was also the first large Matisse retrospective to be held by any museum since 1924, and the first in America. Although Mrs. Rockefeller had not succeeded in converting her husband, she herself had become particularly interested in the artist's most recent work, and she purchased for herself a small oil, not included in the Museum's exhibition. This painting, *Odalisque,* she presented to her son in 1932 when he became a Trustee of the Museum; it was his first significant acquisition of a modern painting.

In that year, the great complex of Rockefeller Center was under construction in New York. Nelson Rockefeller and his mother hoped that Matisse might be persuaded to paint one of the three murals for the large entrance hall of the RCA building. Matisse refused. In 1938, however, Nelson Rockefeller was more successful. He was able to commission a very much smaller, more intimate mural—the overmantle that surrounds a fireplace in his New York apartment. Brightly painted and decorative, it is a gracious and luxurious ornament.

In 1954, Nelson Rockefeller sought Matisse again. His mother had died in 1948, and he asked Matisse to design the stained glass for a memorial rose window in the east wall of the Union Church of Pocantico Hills—the church with which she and her family had been closely associated. Matisse, who remembered Mrs. Rockefeller with affection and respect, accepted the commission. He was not satisfied, however, with the first diagram of the window and its mullions that had been sent to him, and at his request a second, more precise diagram was forwarded to him.

In Nice, on the afternoon of November 2nd, Matisse suffered a fatal heart attack. This distressing news reached New York the following morning. The radio reported that, at the time of his death, the artist had been working on a stained-glass window. Within a week, Mr. Barr received two letters postmarked Nice; the artist had written: "I am very happy to say that this more accurate blueprint reveals a far greater beauty of form than did the preceding scheme....In order not to disturb in any way the spirit of this Protestant chapel, I have avoided employing any kind of symbol, nor have I used geometrical forms or leaves, just as Mr. Rockefeller desired. Dear Mr. Barr...I trust that my work will not disappoint you." In the second letter, Matisse's last, he wrote that he was satisfied: "For me the novelty and the absorbing aspect of this work is the challenge to express myself in a defined and limited space, and to harmonize my composition not only with the form of the actual framework but also with the atmosphere of the chapel." The window with its delicate hues of green, yellow, and blue had been finished. It was installed in the Union Church, where it now has a companion piece—a window which Nelson's youngest brother, David, commissioned ten years later from Marc Chagall, in honor of their father, John D. Rockefeller, Jr.

The two bronzes by Matisse discussed above were both acquired in 1951, after the Second World War, when Nelson Rockefeller's attention had turned increasingly to sculpture. Besides painting and sculpture, he owns several works by Matisse in other media: drawings, among them two of Matisse's finest; and prints, one of which, the marvelously sensuous *Odalisque in Striped Pantaloons*, 1925, is shown here. He has also collected books illustrated by Matisse. One of these volumes is extraordinary. It is Number Twenty-three in an edition of twenty-five of the *Poésies* by Stéphane Mallarmé, 1932, and contains an extra, annotated set of the illustrations. Matisse recalled: "This is the work I completed after reading Mallarmé with pleasure." The subject matter of the twenty-nine etchings, like that of the poems themselves, varies considerably. Without ever being literal, each illustration vividly evokes in a graphic image a specific title or phrase from one of the poems. Matisse chose for his etching needle a sapphire point which, by its very precision, imposes a quick, irrevocable line. The flowing alterations of his draftsmanship create a deceptive effect of effortless spontaneity and lend

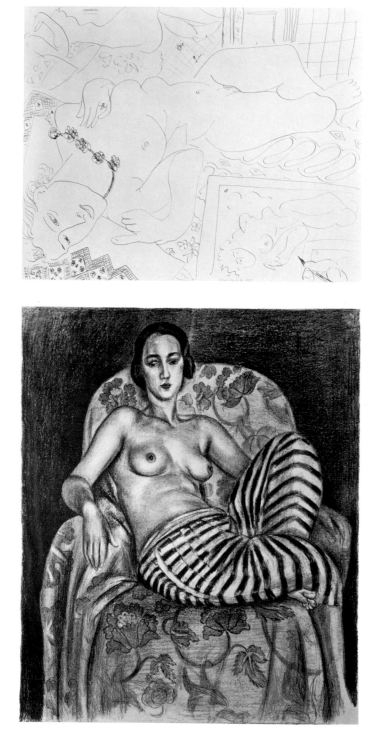

opposite above Matisse. Mural painting, 1938, commissioned for the living room in New York. Andirons are by Giacometti.

opposite below Matisse. The Abby Aldrich Rockefeller Memorial Window. 1954. Union Church of Pocantico Hills, New York

above Matisse. Nude in the Studio. 1935

below Matisse. Odalisque in Striped Pantaloons. 1925

above Picasso. Two Women. 1934

opposite above Rousseau. The Dream. 1910. Gift of Nelson A. Rockefeller to the Museum in 1954

opposite below Matisse. Dance, First Version. 1909. Gift of Nelson A. Rockefeller to the Museum in 1963, in honor of Alfred H. Barr, Jr.

graceful continuity to the pages as they are turned. The varied subjects include images that are new and unexpected in Matisse's art: a swan, and portraits of Edgar Poe and Baudelaire. At least two of the illustrations make reference to Matisse's trip to Tahiti in 1930.

Another Frenchman, Bougainville, in an earlier century had described Tahiti as "la nouvelle Cythère." Matisse's recollection of his own voyage was equally idyllic. An illustration for Mallarmé's poem "Les Fenêtres" appropriately shows a view of the harbor of the island's capital, Papeete, as seen from a window. This etching suggested the theme and design of a cartoon for a tapestry woven three or four years later. The composition of the tapestry, which recalls the earlier landscape, *Collioure* (page 38), is much more elaborate, even baroque, than that of the illustration.

Window at Tahiti is one of a score of tapestries that Mme Marie Cuttoli commissioned from artists of the School of Paris during the 1930s. Picasso's *Two Women* was woven at the same time, from a collage cartoon much more difficult to translate into weaving. Both the Matisse and the Picasso tapestries are included in this exhibition. They are probably the only modern works in Governor Rockefeller's collection which, because of their medium, his father might have found of special interest.

Nelson Rockefeller's reaction to any work of art, like his reaction to people, is immediate, direct, and always interested. He is primarily concerned with the formal elements of an object: its shape, its color, the resolution of its composition. Because he is not particularly attracted by subject matter, there are few paintings in his collection that are descriptive or that invite literary associations. This may explain why he has chosen relatively few surrealist pictures.

Two of his acquisitions, however, are major works that anticipate the painted dreams and illogical juxtapositions of the surrealists. The earlier of these is *The Dream* by *le douanier* Rousseau. Painted in 1910, shortly before the artist's death, it was his last great effort and the consummation of his entire career. Though scorned by the academic critics and laughed at by the public, the paintings of the self-taught Henri Rousseau had qualities that attracted the attention and acclaim of artists as diverse as Degas and Toulouse-Lautrec, the cubists Braque and Picasso (led by the intuitive critic Guillaume Apollinaire), and later the surrealists.

The Dream is Rousseau's tribute in his old age to a Polish school-teacher, Yadwigha, whom he had loved in his youth. When asked to explain the strange scene, Rousseau said: "This woman asleep on the couch dreams that she has been transported into the forest, listening to the sounds from the instruments of the enchanter. That is the reason the couch is in the picture."

First shown in the United States in 1933, *The Dream* was acquired in that year by Sidney Janis for his private collection.

Twenty years later, he told Alfred Barr that he intended to part with it, and would give the Museum the first chance to acquire it. Mr. Barr immediately brought this to the attention of Nelson Rockefeller, then in Washington as Under-Secretary for the Department of Health, Education and Welfare. Mr. Rockefeller, who knew the masterpiece well, deliberated for some time whether to purchase it for his own collection or for the Museum. However, when he discovered that the painting was too large for the wall of his living room in the capital, he generously gave it to the Museum on the occasion of its Twenty-fifth Anniversary in 1954. It has since been seen and enjoyed by millions of visitors.

In 1949, Mr. Rockefeller acquired for his own collection another masterpiece, one of the forerunners of surrealism. This is Giorgio de Chirico's *The Song of Love* (page 10). It was painted in Paris in 1914, when the artist was becoming particularly interested in still life, after having previously created a series of pictures showing silent city squares, peopled only by statues set amid the architecture. In his still lifes, inanimate objects become larger in scale and importance. They are combined in enigmatic juxtapositions whose effect is all the more disquieting because of the realistic manner in which they are painted.

In his monograph on de Chirico, James Thrall Soby wrote of *The Song of Love* that its "insolent and gratuitous juxtaposition of a surgeon's rubber glove with a plaster head of the Apollo Belvedere summarized for many later painters of the surrealist tendency that need for a drastic reshuffling of reality.... The derivation of the glove motif is a rather complex matter.... The glove is a rubber one such as surgeons wear. De Chirico may well have seen its prototype in a pharmacy window, together with the anatomical charts which appear in several of his pictures.... The glove in de Chirico's painting, *The Song of Love*, is also the inanimate protagonist of a fantastic drama, its fellow-actors being a plaster head, a green ball and silent witnesses—architecture and a train.

"De Chirico's still-life drama has no traceable plot, of course; its impact derives from the mystery of assortment of the various elements. But it conveys a considerable sense of shock, and one is again reminded of the words of Guillaume Apollinaire: 'To describe the fatal character of contemporary things, the painter uses that most modern recourse—surprise.' And what makes de Chirico's disruption of conventional reality so memorable in *The Song of Love,* is that it is regulated by a severe, underlying plastic discipline. The counter-logic of the Italian artist's iconography has been imitated by numerous painters but seldom with a conviction comparable to his."

Until shortly before its acquisition by Governor Rockefeller, *The Song of Love* remained in Paris, where it was widely influential among French and Belgian artists. In 1924, ten years after this picture was painted, the French poet André Breton founded surrealism—a movement in literature as well as in the visual arts. Surrealism pursued two courses in exploring the subconscious

above Arp. Man with a Moustache, ca. 1924
opposite above Klee. Sharp Profile. 1924
opposite below Klee. The Jester. 1927

mind. One, following the lead of de Chirico, was illusionistic; to this tendency belong such painters as Ernst, Dali, and Tanguy. An artist who continues this tradition is Paul Delvaux, represented in the exhibition by a much later painting, *The Watchman, II,* 1961 (page 93), and a drawing. The parallel course—free, automatic, and biomorphic—is far more in evidence in Governor Rockefeller's collection.

Jean Arp's lively *Man with a Moustache* of about 1924 is one of a series of compositions, rendered in oil on cardboard with cutouts, which bear no relation whatsoever to illusionism or reality. Arp, who remained the most abstract of the surrealists, reached his full stature with sculpture in the round. His works, although non-representational, nevertheless express the principles of growth and transformation that one finds in nature. By the mid-1930s, Arp had already mastered this style, as for example in the granite *Shell Crystal,* 1938 (page 69). The exhibition also includes several superb examples of his later work in stone (page 68), concrete (page 69), and bronze.

The Catalan artist Joan Miró was a friend and neighbor of Arp's in Montmartre in 1925–26 and was certainly influenced to some extent by the latter's biomorphic inventions. But, like his compatriot Picasso, Miró never thinks of himself as an abstractionist. Two of his paintings in the Rockefeller collection are extraordinary. Both are large in size; one was conceived as a mural, the other as a cartoon for a tapestry. The earlier (page 79) belongs to a series painted in Barcelona in 1933, to which Miró refused to give titles (another of the series is in The Museum of Modern Art). The method of conception was unusual in Miró's art. Before he began to paint, he made preliminary sketches in collage. Such studies, in his own words, "served me as points of departure for paintings. I did not copy the collages. I merely let them suggest shapes to me...." This particularly disciplined work was a self-imposed experiment, a temporary effort to control the automatic spontaneity of his brush. The austere and anchored forms of the final paintings are somber in color.

L'Hirondelle d'amour of 1934 (page 81), a much more joyous song of love than de Chirico's, offers a vivid contrast to Miró's untitled painting of the previous year. Its movements and colors are free; figures, faces, limbs swirl swiftly through the sky, in which Miró also set a star and sun. Although it is difficult for the eye to rest on any single detail, the arrangement of forms is not restless, but graceful and continuously flowing, like the flight of the swallow suggested by the title. The evocative title itself is typically surrealist; here, the calligraphy of its letters is incorporated into the composition. This large painting was one of a series of four cartoons for tapestries by Miró, commissioned, like Matisse's *Window at Tahiti* and Picasso's *Two Women* (page 22), by Mme Marie Cuttoli.

Some of Miró's paintings of the late 1920s have a certain kinship with the art of Paul Klee, to which Miró had been introduced by some of his surrealist colleagues. Although the exquisite clarity of Klee's vision remains independent from that of any of his contemporaries, his inventive fantasy has many affinities with surrealism. James Thrall Soby has described his work as "the chamber music of modern art." Among the Klees in the exhibition are two vivid characterizations of imaginary people, *Sharp Profile* of 1924 and *The Jester,* 1927; and two later paintings, *Fear,* 1934 (page 76) and *Heroic Strokes of the Bow,* 1938 (page 77), which are less literal, and transcend mere description of persons or objects.

"Often," Klee said, "I served Beauty by drawing her enemies, caricature and satire." His *Sharp Profile,* depicting a haughty matron, shares the humorous approach of Arp's witty *Man with a Moustache* of the same year. The technique of Klee's drawing is particularly inventive and is peculiar to his watercolors of the early 1920s. The black lines are "transferred" by placing a sheet of paper over an inked surface and drawing on it with a hard pencil; the pressure of the pencil causes ink to adhere to the verso of the sheet, registering the drawn image in reverse.

The Jester, one of Klee's merriest performers, also presents a "sharp profile." Klee drew and painted several other versions of this figure. Here, the comedian is a juggler; the sharp-edged shapes of the gnomelike tatterdemalion's eye, hand, and costume are set in motion by the circle of five spinning balls.

Fear is painted on burlap. Its pale, hallucinatory image exemplifies several of Klee's theories of form, movement, and line. At the right, fingers of unknown hands reach for the large rounded face, which stares at the unseen assailant with one anxiously fixed eye. This translation into visual terms of a state of mind was painted in the same year that the Nazis seized and burned an edition of a book of Klee's drawings. The artist had already sought refuge in Switzerland a few months before.

Heroic Strokes of the Bow is painted in blue and black. It distills the essence of a specific shape, its motion, and even its sound: the lines simultaneously represent the act of bowing as well as the bow itself. The special music that Klee, the violinist, heard he made visible in the joined lines, curved and straight, that form musical staves. Within this continuous contour, he placed rhythmic beats, notes, and rests. The music is a swelling crescendo. At its close, toward the bottom of the painting, Klee marked the suggestion of a bass clef and a final release.

Alberto Giacometti, whose first sculptural works were strongly influenced by the cubists, came into contact with the surrealists in 1928 and for the next few years participated in their publications and exhibitions. For a long period of time, he continued to alternate between works that explored the unconscious and those more closely related to the visual world and its expression in plastic terms. Three bronzes in the exhibition, made within a ten-year span and all depicting women, reveal various aspects of his art. The pregnant figure, *Spoon Woman,* of 1926 (page 84), is a concave monolith, which in spite of its abstraction is still highly erotic. Its compact curves contrast with the angular, sav-

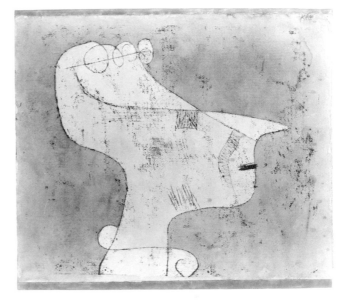

above Lam. Chemical Nuptials. 1944
opposite above Negret. Magical Apparatus, II. 1954
opposite below Eielson. Red Quipu. 1964

agely scattered forms of the *Woman with Her Throat Cut,* 1932 (page 85). This, in turn, is entirely different from the headless *Nude,* 1932–36, a serene, immobile statue that deliberately recalls an archaic style; its attenuation already foreshadows the elongated proportions of Giacometti's later figures, such as those in *City Square,* 1948 (page 86).

In a letter written to Pierre Matisse in 1947, Giacometti recalled some of the contradictions within himself that led to these different phases of his development. After a period in which he had tried to imitate external reality, he found that "It was no longer the exterior forms that interested me but what I really felt....no longer a question of reproducing a lifelike figure but of living, and of executing only what had affected me, or what I really wanted. But all this alternated, contradicted itself, and continued by contrast. There was also a need to find a solution between things that were rounded and calm, and sharp and violent. It was this which led me during those years (32–34 approximately) to objects going in directions that were quite different from each other...I saw anew the bodies that attracted me in reality and the abstract forms which seemed to me true in sculpture, but I wanted to create the former without losing the latter...."

During the Second World War, many artists left Europe for the United States, some as temporary refugees and others to remain. Several of them were surrealists—Ernst, Masson, Tanguy, Dali, and Matta among them. Their influence was especially important for the birth of the style that developed in New York during the 1940s and came to be known as "abstract expressionism" or "the new American painting." A focus for the showing of many of these European artists and for the young Americans whose own styles were just beginning to emerge was Peggy Guggenheim's gallery, Art of This Century, which opened in 1942 and was designed by Frederick Kiesler. This Vienna-born architect, designer, and sculptor, who had come to the United States as a theater designer in 1926, had been associated with a succession of avant-garde movements since the early 1920s, and remained a pioneer until his death in 1965, at age seventy-five. Among the most successful of his ambitious projects, articulated through the language of surrealism, is the large and stunning *Galaxy* (page 101). Kiesler, who had made an earlier version of this construction, completed the final work in 1951; it was first exhibited at The Museum of Modern Art in 1952, in *15 Americans,* an exhibition organized by Dorothy Miller. This unforgettable structure was reproduced in *Harper's Bazaar* (April 1952) and described by Lily Auchincloss as "a spatial sculpture...made of wood fashioned only with a saw and joined with wooden pegs. It measures twelve feet high, and the length of its longest crossbar is over fourteen feet. Kiesler...looks on *Galaxy* as a practical sculpture, to live with and within—to put in a garden, in a wooded grove or on a beach." In the same periodical Alfred Barr did more than describe the construction; he composed a poem. Within the posts of the wooden frame, Mr. Barr visualized four sailors, one flown, one swallowed, one shipwrecked, and the last damned:

"*Galaxy* is architecture for sky-gazers; its plan is a cross with arms raised in amazement; its major axis slopes abruptly toward a vanishing point like Borromini's false perspective in the Palazzo Spada; its four caryatids are a dolphin's spine, a hippocampus, a lobster claw and an ichthyosaur caressed by a boomerang; its lintels are driftwood and a comb-finned gar.

"*Galaxy* is a four-poster in which Sinbad, Jonah, Crusoe and Ahab may sit eternally, back to back, telling each other their stories, slowly, with low voices and credulous ears.

"*Galaxy* is a pergola built of jetsam where refugees from the compass and ruler may dry their nets in peace.

"*Galaxy* is a drifting raft where common sense, watched by the skeletons of the four winds, will die of thirst.

"*Galaxy* is a conspiracy for discrediting Cadillacs.

"*Galaxy* is the tomb of know-how, the supreme antitechnological gazebo."

Among the artists who left France during the war was Wifredo Lam, who returned to his native Cuba in 1941. After his early studies in Havana, Lam had lived first in Spain and then in Paris. There he met Picasso, who aided and deeply influenced him; and there, also, he joined the surrealist group. As in many of Lam's works, *Chemical Nuptials,* 1944, retains the exotic atmosphere of the semi-tropics; it is an heraldic allegory that disquietingly marries birds and flowers.

Lam's painting is one of a number of works by Latin American artists in Governor Rockefeller's collection. During the 1930s, he and his mother had become familiar with the work of the great Mexican muralists and had been responsible for commissioning murals from two of them, Rivera and Orozco. In 1940, while still president of The Museum of Modern Art, he was appointed Coordinator of Inter-American Affairs by the federal government. He held this position until 1944, when he became Assistant Secretary of State. In Washington, Mr. Rockefeller instituted and carried out broad programs to foster understanding among the American republics. Characteristically, some of them involved the arts.

In 1942, in a private capacity, he enabled The Museum of Modern Art to initiate the formation of a collection devoted to Latin American art. In this he was aided by Lincoln Kirstein, then impresario of the American Ballet Caravan. During a twenty-eight-week tour of South America, Kirstein "scouted" an impressive group of paintings, drawings, and prints. In the same year, Alfred Barr and Edgar Kaufmann, Jr. bought for the Museum in Cuba and Mexico. In 1943, this large collection, perhaps the first of its kind to be assembled, was shown at the Museum, together with Latin American works which it had previously acquired. Nelson Rockefeller established a recurrent Inter-American Fund, through which the Museum has continued to make significant additions to this special collection.

above Tobey. Voyagers, III. 1954

opposite above Gorky. The Calendars. 1946–47. Destroyed by fire in the Governor's Mansion in 1961

opposite below Pollock. Number 12, 1952. Partially destroyed by fire in the Governor's Mansion in 1961

Governor Rockefeller's own interest in the arts of the Latin American republics has also continued, and the exhibition includes several examples from his private collection: *St. John's Day,* 1938 (page 92), by the Mexican painter Julio Castellanos; the sculpture *Magical Apparatus, II,* 1954 (page 27), by Edgar Negret of Colombia; a work of 1964 in tempera and knotted cloth on canvas by the Peruvian Jorge Eielson, called *Red Quipu* (page 27); and pieces by Emilio Rodriguez-Larrain y Balta, also from Peru; Rogelio Polesello of Argentina; and the Uruguayan Antonio Frasconi.

This exhibition displays, eloquently and selectively, a choice from the broad panorama of painting in the United States since the Second World War. It also reveals Governor Rockefeller's personal preference for abstract expressionism; indeed, during the 1950s he was one of the foremost collectors of the movement. He acquired the paintings by William Baziotes, James Brooks, Helen Frankenthaler, Adolph Gottlieb, Philip Guston, Grace Hartigan, Willem de Kooning, Mark Rothko, and Mark Tobey shown in this exhibition in the very years in which they were painted or first exhibited. In 1950 and 1952, Mr. Rockefeller bought paintings by Jackson Pollock. He gave *Number 16, 1950* to the Museu de Arte Moderna in Rio de Janeiro; another, *Number 12, 1952,* was one of Pollock's masterpieces.

There is a tragic reason for the absence from this exhibition of that painting, and of three others of prime importance in the development of abstract expressionism: Arshile Gorky's *The Calendars,* 1946–47; Franz Kline's *Corinthian,* 1957; and Bradley Walker Tomlin's *Number 18,* 1950. On the night of March 6, 1961, when Nelson Rockefeller had been Governor of the State of New York for two years, fire swept the Executive Mansion in Albany. Fortunately, lives were spared; but some of his favorite paintings and prints were completely destroyed or badly damaged. The loss among his American paintings was particularly severe, for the four highly important pictures just named, as well as others, were among those burnt.

From the point of view of its significance for the development of abstract expressionism, perhaps the most serious of these losses was that of Gorky's *The Calendars.* Gorky was born in Armenia, and came to the United States when he was sixteen. Though his early style was modeled upon a succession of painters as disparate as Ingres, Cézanne, and Picasso, among others, he may be regarded as an authentic disciple of surrealism. He came to know this movement in the 1930s through his friend, the dealer Julien Levy, who had long been its chief American propagandist; during the war years Gorky was close to the surrealists who found refuge in the United States, including Breton himself, as well as the artists Ernst, Tanguy, Masson, and Matta. Incidentally, the first magazine article on Gorky—a discussion of his murals, now lost, executed for the Newark Airport under the WPA Federal Art Project—was written by Frederick Kiesler.

In 1942, Gorky's art reached maturity. As the combined influences of Picasso, Miró, and Matta were absorbed, and as his style became increasingly defined in technique and imagery, his own vision was finally released. The large pictures done in 1946 and 1947, a year or so before his death, achieve a kind of heroic nobility. Among the most important of them was the five-foot-wide, opaquely colored *Calendars,* which Governor Rockefeller acquired in 1950.

Gorky was a meticulous craftsman and usually made detailed studies on paper for his paintings. Although no specific drawing for *The Calendars* is known, a smaller, preliminary oil painting exists. *The Calendars* transforms an interior—a living room or studio—into an abstraction. The defined areas of space within the composition can be easily described: in the center foreground, a diagonal thrust; in the background, vertical planes of different colors. A table in the foreground displays a still life; above it, near the upper right corner of the painting, is a lampshade. An easel set with a picture appears at the left. In another room, at the right, a figure sits at some sort of drawing table. In the center of the canvas, an ovoid shape contains forms that may suggest burning logs. Gorky repeated the elements of this composition at least twice, in two smaller pictures of 1947 painted in more diaphanous, liquid hues, *Making the Calendar* (Munson-Williams-Proctor Institute, Utica) and *Days, etc.* (collection of Mr. and Mrs. Julien Levy). The seated figure appears again in *The Orators,* also of 1947 (collection of Mr. and Mrs. William C. Janss), transposed into the central speaker.

The loss of *The Calendars* was all the more regrettable, because in 1946 about twenty-seven of Gorky's paintings in his studio in Connecticut had also been destroyed by fire. In June 1948, he committed suicide—the victim of illness, personal misfortunes, and what he regarded as a lack of adequate recognition of his contribution as an artist. In fact, full appreciation of Gorky's originality and his influence on the formation of the "new American painting" did not come until after his death, even though he had had one-man shows at the Julien Levy Gallery each year beginning in 1945, and in 1946 was significantly represented by eight paintings and two drawings in The Museum of Modern Art's exhibition *Fourteen Americans,* organized by Dorothy Miller.

As tragic as the loss of *The Calendars* was that of Jackson Pollock's *Number 12, 1952,* for the artist, like Gorky, was no longer living, and the destroyed painting was unique in his work. Early in 1952, Pollock had become dissatisfied with the series of large paintings in black enamel on white, unsized canvas, on which he had been engaged for some time. In revolt against the self-imposed discipline of black and white, he completely repainted two of these pictures by covering their surfaces with color. Understandably, the impasto of both paintings, *Blue Poles* and *Convergence,* is thick; but Pollock's next large composition, *Number 12, 1952,* was much more thinly painted on a clean can-

above Glarner. Mural paintings, 1964, commissioned for the dining room in New York

opposite Nevelson. White Column from "Dawn's Wedding Feast." 1959

vas, expressing his resolve to return to color. The easy continuity of its lines displayed the relaxed control of his previous black-and-white pictures, but this was the only large canvas in which Pollock composed broad areas of thinly washed colors. Skeins of liquid black played against great pools of almost pretty colors, whose transparency was heightened by glimpses of the dulled silver of aluminum paint. The contrast between the black lines and the limpid veils of color implied a limitless space; like many of Pollock's late works, *Number 12, 1952* was universal in concept, and was stated with dynamic intensity. Almost oriental in mood, this work on canvas, like Chinese or Japanese paintings on paper, was a masterful consummation of draftsmanship for painterly effect.

Bradley Walker Tomlin, too, was dead when the fire in the Executive Mansion destroyed his painting *Number 18,* 1950. Fortunately Governor Rockefeller was able to secure an earlier and not too dissimilar work by him, *Number 5* of 1949 (page 107). Of the four major abstract expressionists whose work was lost, only Kline was still alive. He was naturally extremely distressed by the destruction of a picture that he considered one of his best; after some hesitation, he painted a second version, *Corinthian, II,* 1961 (page 109). By the following year, Kline, too, was dead.

Included in this exhibition are paintings by several other artists deeply committed to abstract expressionism: Adolph Gottlieb, Robert Motherwell, and Mark Rothko; William Baziotes, James Brooks, Philip Guston, and Morris Louis; and, of a second generation, Helen Frankenthaler and Grace Hartigan.

In selecting contemporary American paintings, however, Nelson Rockefeller has in no way limited his choices to abstract expressionism. He has purchased works by many other Americans—again, shortly after they were painted. Among those shown here are examples of Jasper Johns's long celebration of the alchemy of numbers, including one of his most eloquent (page 111). An early striped painting by Frank Stella and his heraldic tondo of 1968 (page 119) are joined by hard-edged paintings by Fritz Glarner, Alexander Liberman, and Ellsworth Kelly, as well as by more disparate companions, such as Peter Dechar's inflated image, *Pear,* and Charles Hinman's three-dimensional shaped canvas.

Two of Governor Rockefeller's architect friends have helped him modify his house and apartment to accommodate more works of art. As the dining room in New York was being remodeled, Wallace Harrison suggested that it be redone completely with murals on the walls and ceiling—a practice more frequent in former times than today. This commission was entrusted to Fritz Glarner and resulted in an excellent environment. Philip Johnson, whom Nelson Rockefeller had first met in the 1930s as a member of the Museum's Advisory Committee, helped him add the space he needed for the recent works he was constantly acquiring. Mr. Johnson's solution was a long gallery, recently constructed at a lower level of the house at

Pocantico Hills. The walls of this special room, almost 12 feet wide and 140 feet long, can accommodate large contemporary paintings and constructions. The gallery gradually descends underground, and opens—to a visitor's considerable astonishment—into a fantastic grotto, a splendid architectural folly of an older generation, which in turn opens onto a lower garden.

In sculpture, as in painting, Governor Rockefeller's collection demonstrates his particular interest in advanced developments of the past two decades. He has, however, acquired a number of stellar works belonging to the previous fifty years, many of which have already been discussed. From the last decade of the nineteenth century, he owns only two examples: a small bronze study by Rodin, and, by Maillol, a bronze *Bather,* enlarged to life size in 1930 from a small terra cotta of 1898 (page 36). Two additional bronzes by Maillol, the pensive *Night* (page 37) and the dynamic *Chained Action,* date from this century's first years. Although expressed in naturalistic terms, the underlying aesthetic of the latter work is not unlike that of Duchamp-Villon's *Horse.*

Governor Rockefeller has devoted particular attention to three American sculptors, each born before 1900, each highly individual in style: Gaston Lachaise and Elie Nadelman, both of whom left France to live in the United States, and Alexander Calder, who, in turn, now resides in France. At the Beaux-Arts in Paris, Lachaise had received a thorough academic training; and when he came to New York, he worked for a time as assistant to Paul Manship, a successful and highly favored sculptor who was the master of a somewhat lifeless pseudo-classic style. The exuberant vitality of Lachaise's art, however, was far removed from official taste. Obsessive deification of the opulent female form is central to his work. His heroic women overpower the spectator, and each dominating figure is, as well, a mother image. In spite of their often frank eroticism, these figures do not entice; they are idols, objects of awe.

In 1935, a few months before Lachaise died, Lincoln Kirstein directed a retrospective exhibition of his sculpture and drawings for The Museum of Modern Art. Nelson Rockefeller had already begun to collect bronzes by Lachaise, who had also been among the artists commissioned for the decoration of Rockefeller Center. Mr. Rockefeller's interest in the sculptor's work has continued, and as recently as 1967 he bought the majestic *Standing Woman* (page 71), the most elegant of Lachaise's over-life-sized figures, which had been completed forty years before.

Born in Poland in 1882, the same year as Lachaise, Nadelman studied in Warsaw and Munich and worked for several years in France before arriving in the United States in 1914, shortly after the outbreak of the war. Original in style, he had been associated in Paris with the modern movement, in which he was influential, and numbered among his patrons Gertrude and Leo Stein. In New York, he soon established contact with the few Americans interested in advanced art, had a show at Stieglitz's "291" Gal-

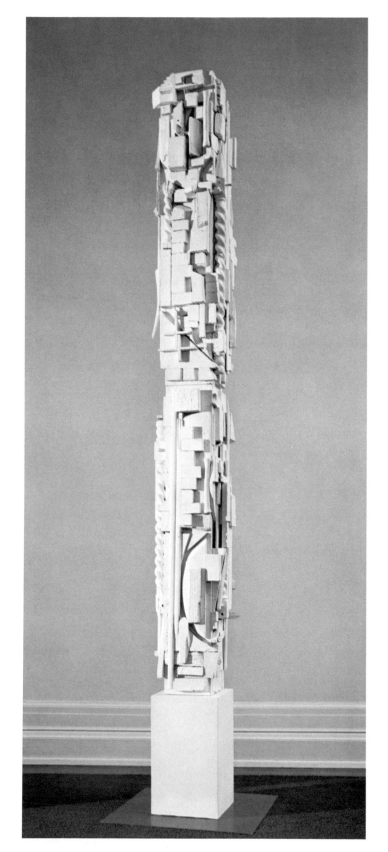

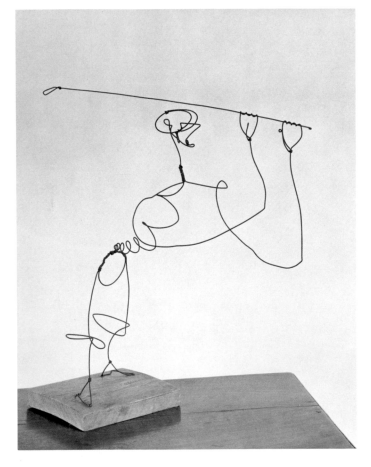

above Nadelman. Standing Bull. 1915
below Calder. The Golfer (John D. Rockefeller, Sr.). ca. 1928

lery, and exhibited frequently thereafter, attaining considerable artistic and social success. During the last decades of his life, however, Nadelman became a recluse. He continued to produce but refused either to exhibit or sell. By the time of his death in 1946, he was almost forgotten. In 1948, a large Nadelman retrospective, also organized by Lincoln Kirstein, was held at the Museum and led to an unexpected revaluation of his achievement. Nelson Rockefeller, however, remembered the artist well, and he remains particularly fond of his sculpture. He has said: "He was a curious and wonderful man. My mother bought a great deal of her collection of American folk art from the Nadelmans.... What interests me ... apart from the beauty and the wit of his pieces, is his very democratic concept of making many of his sculptures in *papier-mâché,* with the idea that they would be more financially available to the public."

Nelson Rockefeller owns some thirty of these doll-like, curiously proportioned figurines; they are scattered and constantly rearranged in his official residence in Albany, his house in Pocantico Hills, and his apartment in New York. He has also collected several bronzes by Nadelman, of which the earliest is the *Standing Bull* of 1915, an intense work, aggressively modeled. The other bronzes are later in date and larger in size: a pair of relaxed seated "circus women" (page 70), and two larger groups of two figures each, cast posthumously from originals in *papier-mâché.* Greatly enlarged versions of the latter two groups were also posthumously carved in marble for the promenade of the New York State Theater in Lincoln Center. The attitudes of these graces are bemused, their forms soft and sometimes veiled, the surfaces ideally curved and sensuous.

Alexander Calder has been a friend of Nelson Rockefeller's for many years. From a number of Calders in his collection, this exhibition includes two mobile constructions of 1949 and 1961 (page 82), and two stabiles (pages 82–83), one an enlargement, twelve feet high, of a small, perfect work cut and welded almost a quarter of a century before.

Nelson Rockefeller particularly appreciates light-hearted humor and its rendering in three-dimensional objects. He owns several such pieces, usually in fragile media, and his associations with them are very personal. In his bedroom he keeps a Calder drawing in wire, one of the artist's wittiest portraits of the late 1920s. Calder had mislaid this small caricature of John D. Rockefeller, Sr. as a golfer, but when he found it again in 1958, he gave it to the subject's grandson. Other objects, equally quick in their humor, include Isamu Noguchi's terra cotta *Mr. One-Man* of 1952, which sits on the Governor's desk in Albany; and in his home in Pocantico Hills, an "arrange-it-yourself" of plaster forms on strings by Yasuhide Kobashi, and two painted ceramic birds —an owl and a condor—by Picasso, both in the exhibition. A less intimate work, but similarly humorous, is Picasso's extraordinary group. *The Bathers* (page 65), which brings together six flat and angular mannequins, each cast in bronze from constructions assembled mostly of wood planks, with, paradoxically, as much insouciance as care.

Today, sculpture is the most rapidly expanding part of Nelson Rockefeller's collection. As might be expected, he owns several classic and imposing examples in stone and bronze, which are traditionally carved or cast, by masters such as Arp, Moore, and Noguchi. Among these are two of Moore's great bronzes of the 1960s, *Knife Edge Two Piece* (page 75), one of the sculptor's most splendid achievements, and *Nuclear Energy* (page 74), the smaller version of the twelve-foot monument commissioned for the site on the campus of the University of Chicago where the atom was first split in underground laboratories (now destroyed). Noguchi's *Black Sun,* carved in granite (page 117), has also been enlarged to monumental scale and will occupy a site in front of the art museum in Seattle, Washington.

Increasingly, however, Nelson Rockefeller seeks works by sculptors whose reputations have developed more recently, and who do not hesitate to work with less conventional materials. Some of these works are of extraordinary size, and of a scale that commands much space for their installation. An extreme example is the five-part *Wandering Rocks* by Tony Smith (pages 126–127), which, like Clement Meadmore's *U Turn* (page 123), is almost a landscape in itself.

Contemporary American sculpture is particularly well represented in the collection. There are two masterpieces in steel by David Smith: one of his "drawings in space," *The Banquet* of 1951 (page 102), and the huge *Voltri VI,* one of the prolific series welded in Italy in 1962 (page 103). In some respects, Smith's sculpture parallels the painting of the abstract expressionists, as do, still more closely, works by some other artists included in the exhibition: by Herbert Ferber, in copper (page 105); by Ibram Lassaw, in lead over copper (page 106); and two pieces, of steel and other metals, by Seymour Lipton—*The Cloak,* 1952 (page 100), a vertical and visceral metaphor, and the *Storm Bird,* 1953, a horizontal creature, alert and poised for flight. The sculptor Louise Nevelson might also be considered a counterpart to the abstract expressionist painters, especially in such a work as the white, painted wood construction (page 31), two parts of a larger assemblage originally designed to fill a room. Nevelson is also represented in the exhibition by two more recent architectonic constructions, an aluminum wall (page 116) and a small plexiglass object, which invite the eye to penetrate their laddered open spaces.

The work of these sculptors—David Smith excepted—was first introduced to a wide public through the series of exhibitions devoted to American artists that Dorothy Miller directed at The Museum of Modern Art. Three other sculptors so presented are also included in the collection. In conception and execution, there is no similarity among the works of these artists, and indeed all three stand somewhat apart from their American contemporaries. The shimmering, linear tension of Richard Lip-

above Noguchi. Mr. One-Man. 1952
below Picasso. Red and White Owl. 1953

Picasso. Minotauromachy. 1935

pold's taut *Bird of Paradise* in gold offers a complete contrast to Raoul Hague's *Annandale-on-Hudson* (page 104), carved of solid walnut. Robert Mallary's *Head of a Bull* expressively lends to humble materials, composition stone and resin, a poetry that is lonely, tragic, and abandoned.

Younger American sculptors in the exhibition work in even more varied media, and in modes of expression that could only have been conceived today. Larry Bell and Lee Bontecou have each created completely different abstract poems—the former a delicately tinted, precisely designed glass cube, the other a canvas and metal construction with a mysterious, asymmetrically placed round aperture (page 113). Less concerned with mood are the welded sculptures of Jason Seley and Richard Stankiewicz, which transform scrap metal into elegant assemblages, and a remarkable piece, *Granny's Knot* (page 125), by Shinkichi Tajiri, now working in the Netherlands.

Although Nelson Rockefeller's collection of contemporary sculpture represents his personal choice and makes no attempt to be comprehensive, it is nevertheless a broad international selection. Among the many works by foreign artists, for example, are those by four British sculptors younger than Moore—Kenneth Armitage, Reg Butler, Lynn Chadwick, and Eduardo Paolozzi; by three Italian sculptors, Umberto Mastroianni, Arnaldo Pomodoro, and Francesco Somaini; by Masayuke Nagare of Japan; and by artists resident in Paris—Pol Bury, Horst-Egon Kalinowski, and Jean Ipousteguy; as well as many others.

Japanese prints collected by his mother were among the first works of art that Nelson Rockefeller, many years ago, touched and studied. Some of them she gave to the Philadelphia Museum of Art; a few others, her son requested for himself. In 1927, she also promised him Toulouse-Lautrec's lithograph, *Ride in the Country;* he himself later added other lithographs by Lautrec, several of which were destroyed by the fire in the Executive Mansion. He also owns complete sets of *L'Epreuve* and *L'Estampe originale,* which contain original prints in various media by artists of the late nineteenth century: Bernard, Bonnard, Carrière, Denis, Gauguin, Pissarro, Redon, Renoir, Rodin, Toulouse-Lautrec, Vallotton, Vuillard, and Whistler. Today it is rare, indeed almost impossible, to discover these sets intact, as issued.

Before becoming governor, Mr. Rockefeller had more time to devote to his collection of prints and illustrated books. He acquired thirty-three prints by Picasso, including the great *Minotauromachy,* and in addition the complete suite of one hundred etchings issued, after Vollard's death in 1939, from plates that Picasso had traded with him for paintings by Renoir and other modern masters. More recent acquisitions include books illustrated by artists as different as Braque, Glarner, and Bontecou. His holdings of printed works might furnish the contents for a separate exhibition; their range can barely be indicated by the small selection shown here.

In private and in public life, the man who owns these paintings, sculptures, drawings, and prints runs counter to the tradition set by most American statesmen. As a connoisseur, he is thoroughly acquainted with the broad span of modern art; he is also a champion of his own time and of the future. This is complemented by his own special appreciation, aesthetic rather than ethnographic, of the artifacts of primitive societies.

As a collector, he is determined and audacious. He knows that what he needs from himself is an immediate response; he is interested in what a work looks like, not what it represents. Once acquired, the work is subjected to constant scrutiny, as he studies its construction, pattern, and formal relationships.

Nelson Rockefeller is never so happy and relaxed as when he can act as his own curator, hanging paintings or placing sculpture. Whenever he installs, he insists on touching and physically moving the object himself, often to his associates' dismay. In addition, he is by far the most eloquent docent for his own collection, as those who have heard him can testify.

The collection, considered as a general survey of modern art, naturally has some fascinating omissions, because the choice of treasures is so personal. But it remains one of the most glorious ever assembled. The Museum of Modern Art is proud to have the opportunity to show it, through a comprehensive selection, for the first time.

left Maillol. Bather Putting Up Her Hair. 1930. Bronze, 61½″ high

opposite Maillol. Night. 1902–09. Bronze, 41½″ high

above Matisse. Collioure. 1911. Oil, 24¾ x 20⅜″
opposite Matisse. Italian Woman. 1915. Oil, 45¾ x 35¼″

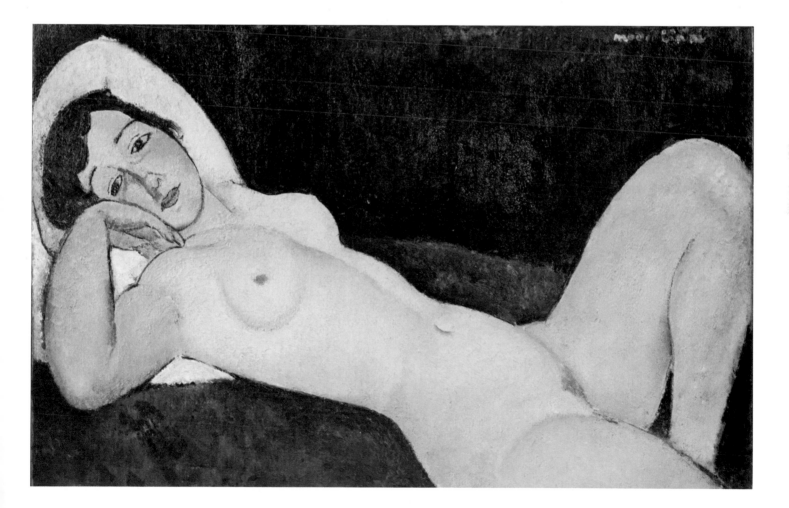

opposite above Matisse. Reclining Nude, I. 1907. Bronze, 13½″ high
opposite below Matisse. Seated Nude. 1925. Bronze, 31½″ high
above Modigliani. The Dreamer. 1918. Oil, 23½″ x 36¼″

Kandinsky. Autumn Landscape, Murnau. 1908. Oil, 27¼ x 37¼"

Jawlensky. The Spanish Girl. 1912. Oil, 27 x 19¼ ″

above van Dongen. Woman in a Large Hat. 1908. Oil, 39½″ x 32″
opposite above   Lehmbruck. Dancer. 1913–14. Cast stone, 11½″ high
opposite below Lehmbruck. Torso. 1910. Cast stone, 45″ high

above Picasso. Harvesters. 1907. Oil, 25½ x 32″
opposite Picasso. Girl with a Mandolin (Fanny Tellier). 1910. Oil, 39½ x 29″

opposite above Picasso. Still Life: Le Torero. 1911. Oil, 19¼ x 15⅛″

opposite below Picasso. Still Life: ''Job.'' 1916. Oil, 17 x 13¼″

above Braque. Clarinet. 1913. Pasted papers, charcoal, chalk, and oil, 37½ x 47⅜″

Braque. Guitar, Newspaper, and Bottle. 1913–14. Oil, 28⅞ x 21¼"

Gris. Guitar, Bottle, and Glass. 1914. Pasted papers, gouache, and crayon, 36⅛ x 25½"

Boccioni. States of Mind. 1911.
opposite above Those Who Go. Oil, 27⅞ x 37¾"
opposite below Those Who Stay. Oil, 27⅞ x 37¾"
below The Farewells. Oil, 27¾ x 37⅞"

opposite Duchamp-Villon.
The Horse (Le Cheval majeur).
1914 (second enlarged version, 1966). Bronze, 59″ high

right Gris. The Sideboard.
1917. Oil, 46⅞″ x 28¾″

above Léger. Armistice. 1918. Oil, 21¾ x 15"
opposite Léger. Woman with a Book. 1923. Oil, 45½ x 32"

58

left Lipchitz. Seated Man with Guitar. 1922. Granite, 15⅞″ high
right Archipenko. Standing Woman. 1923. Mahogany, 17½″ high
opposite Braque. The Table. 1930. Oil and sand, 57⅝ x 30⅜″

above Mondrian. Large Composition A. 1919. Oil, 35½ x 35¾″
opposite Brancusi. Bird in Space. 1926? White marble, 6′2⅜″ high

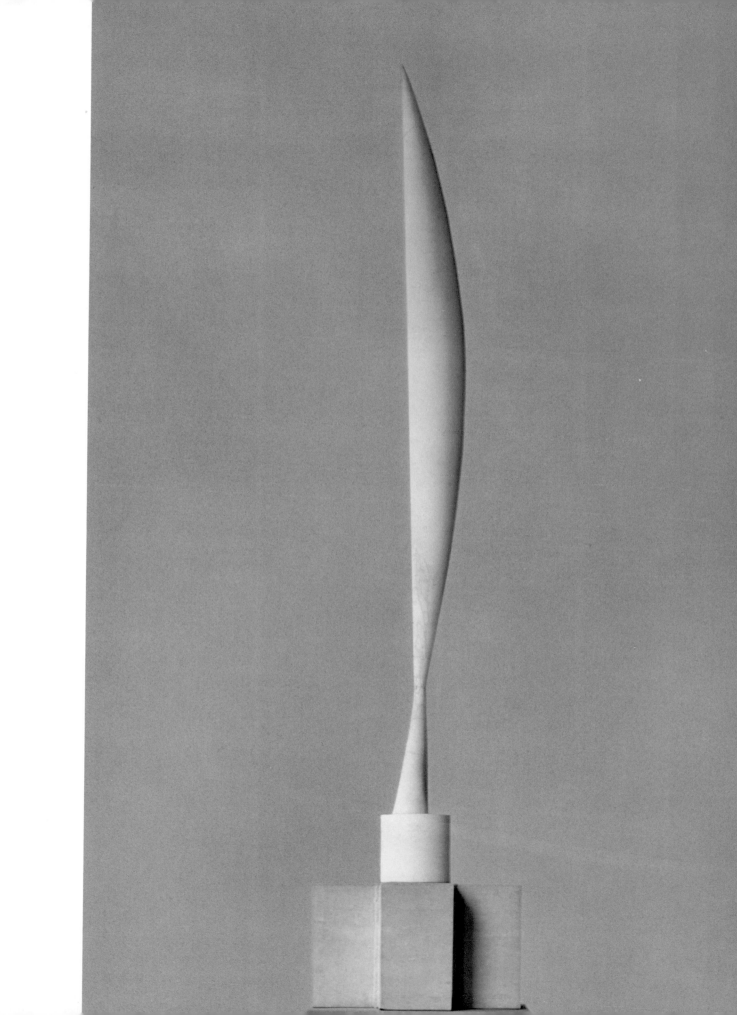

opposite Picasso. Pitcher and Bowl of Fruit. 1931. Oil, 51½ x 64″
above Picasso. Interior with a Girl Drawing. 1935. Oil, 51⅛ x 6′4⅝″

above Picasso. The Striped Bodice. 1943. Oil, 39⅜ x 32⅛″
opposite Picasso. The Bathers. 1956. Bronze, after wood. Tallest figure, 8′8″ high

below Gonzalez. Reclining Figure. 1934. Wrought iron, 17¾″ high
opposite Gabo. Construction in Space, X. 1952–53. Plexiglass and nylon wire, 28″ high

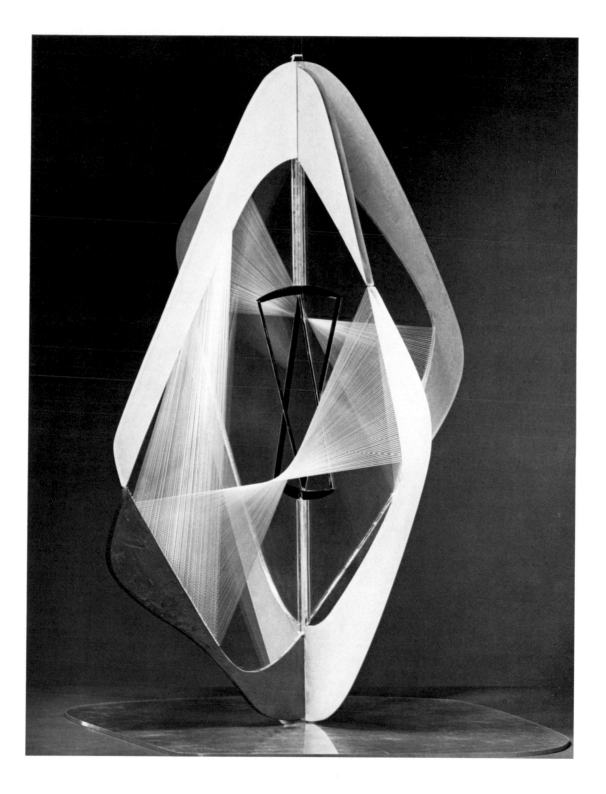

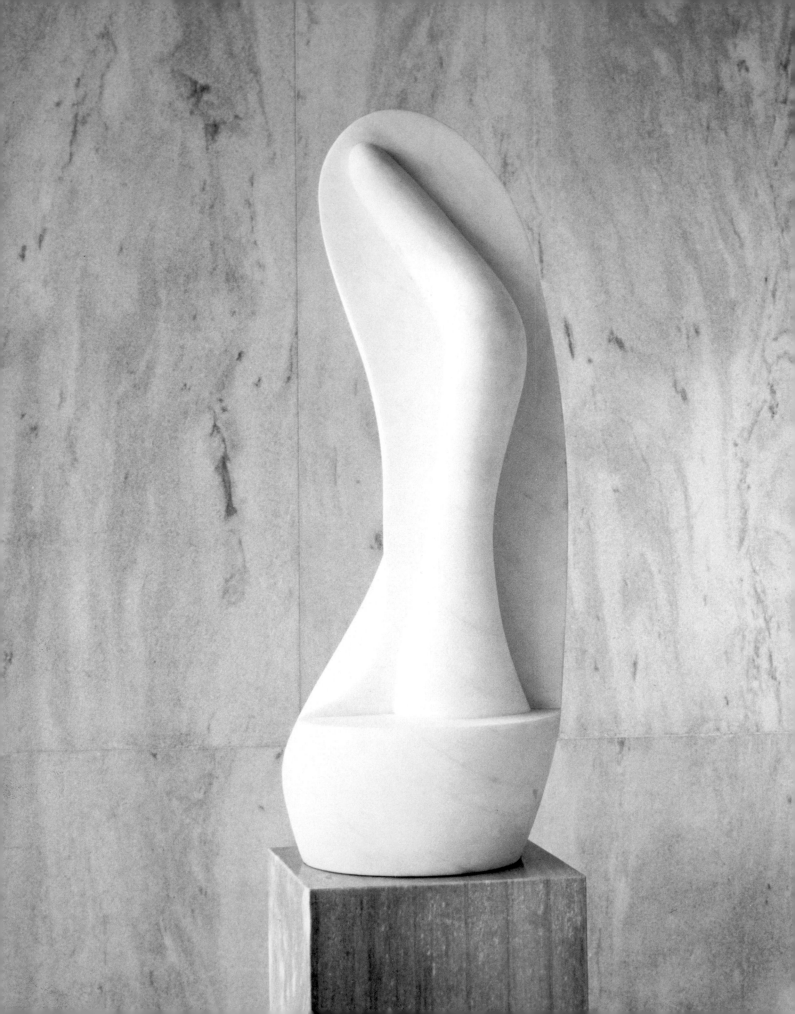

opposite Arp. Amphora of the Muse. 1959. Marble, 44¾″ high

above Arp. Shell Crystal. 1938. Granite, 13″ high

below Arp. Snake Movement, II. 1955. Concrete, 16¼ x 28 x 23¼″

left Nadelman. Circus Woman, I. ca. 1924. Bronze, 49¼″ high
right Nadelman. Circus Woman, II. ca. 1924. Bronze, 44¾″ high
opposite Lachaise. Standing Woman. 1927. Bronze, 70½″ high

above Moore. King and Queen. 1952. Bronze, 10¾ x 8¼″
below Lachaise. Torso. 1932. Bronze, 7⅝″ high
opposite Moore. Family Group. 1948–49. Bronze, 59¼ x 46½″

74

above Moore. Nuclear Energy. 1964. Bronze, 45½″ high
opposite Moore. Knife Edge Two Piece. 1962 (large version 1965–66). Bronze, 9 x 12′

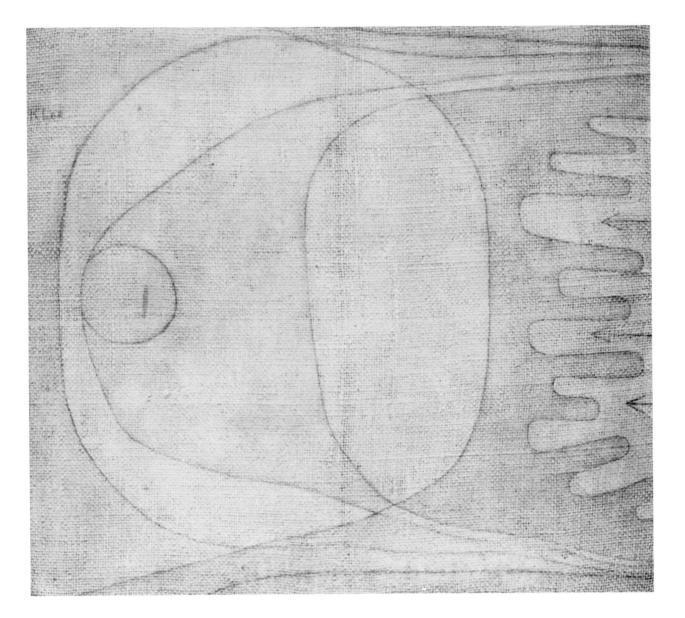

above Klee. Fear. 1934. Oil, 19¾ x 21¾″
opposite Klee. Heroic Strokes of the Bow. 1938. Tempera, 28¾ x 20⅞″

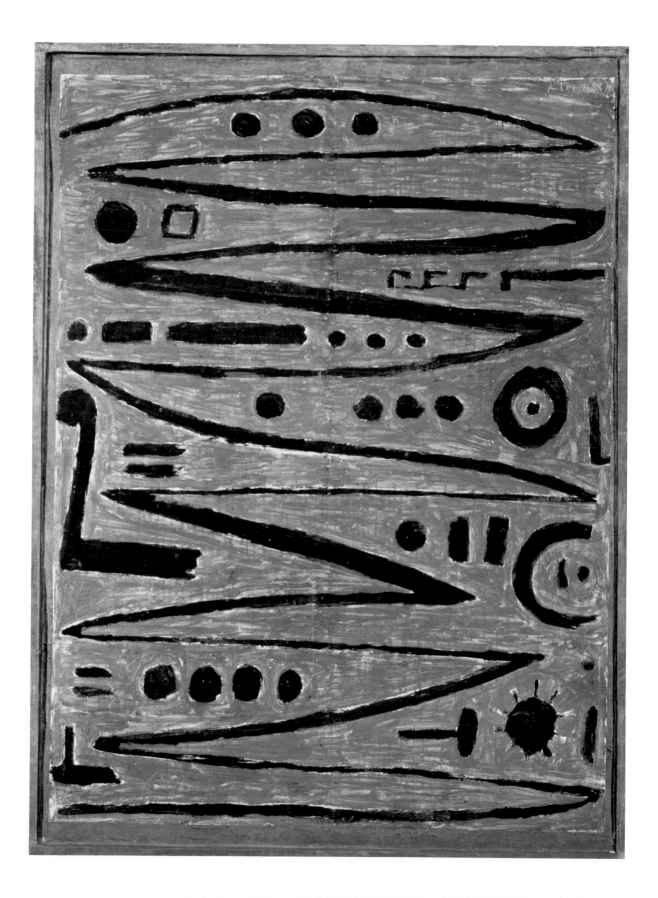

Kurt Schwitters 1928

opposite above Schwitters. ''Vollmilch.'' 1928. Pasted papers, 5⅜ x 4⅛ ″
opposite below Schwitters. Merz 212: ''Detektiv-K....'' 1921. Pasted papers, 7⅛ x 5⅝ ″
above Miró. Painting. 1933. Oil, 51¼ ″ x 6′5 ″

above Miró. Collage. 1933. Pasted papers, charcoal, pencil, and ink on sandpaper, 42¾ x 28⅛"

opposite Miró. L'Hirondelle d'amour. 1934. Oil, 6'6½" x 8'1½"

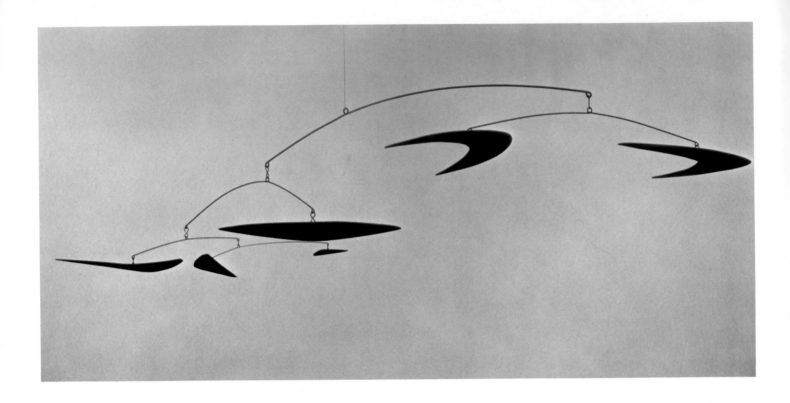

above Calder. Flying Boomerangs. 1961. Steel, 9′8″ wide
below Calder. Spiny. 1942. Aluminum, 26″ high
opposite Calder. Large Spiny. 1966 (after stabile of 1942). Steel, 12′6″ high

opposite Giacometti. Spoon Woman. 1926. Bronze, 57″ high
below Giacometti. Woman with Her Throat Cut. 1932. Bronze, 34½″ long

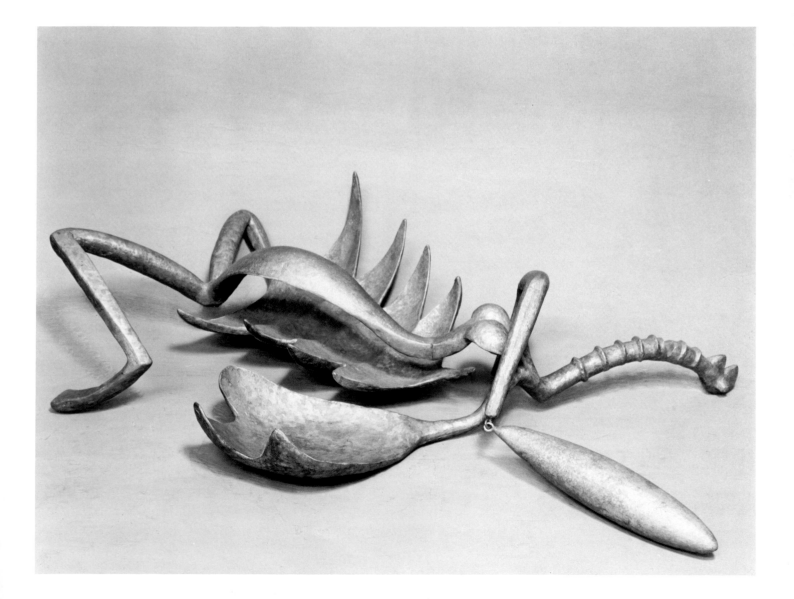

Giacometti. City Square. 1948. Bronze, 8½ x 25⅜ x 17¼″

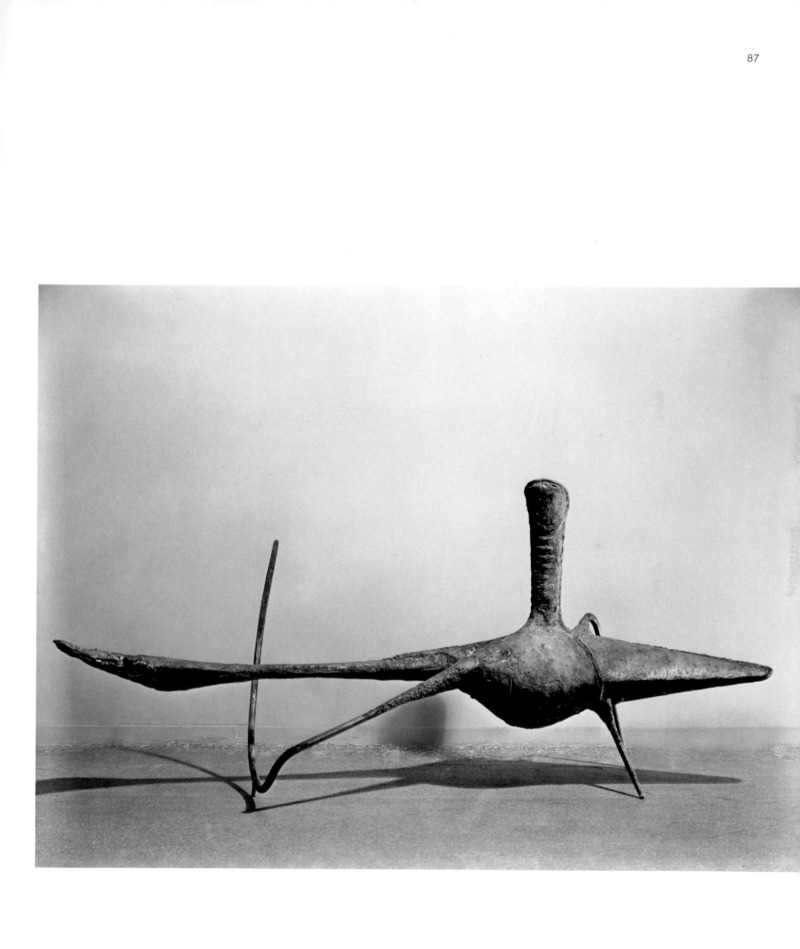

Butler. Oracle. 1952. Cast shell bronze, 33½″ x 6′1″ x 35½″

opposite Butler. Manipulator. 1954. Cast shell bronze, 67″ high
below Ipousteguy. Alexander before Ecbatane. 1965. Bronze, 68″ x 12′

opposite Beckmann. Woman with a Parrot. 1946. Oil, 37¼ x 23¾″
above Morandi. Still Life. 1939. Oil, 17⅛ x 20¾″

opposite above Castellanos. St. John's Day. 1938. Oil, 15¾ x 18⅞″
opposite below Blume. Excavation. 1945. Oil, 21⅛ x 27″
below Delvaux. The Watchman, II. 1961. Oil, 48″ x 8′

opposite Gottlieb. Transfiguration. 1958. Oil, 7′6″ x 60″
above Motherwell. Granada: Elegy to the Spanish Republic, II. 1949. Oil, 48 x 56⅛″

opposite de Kooning. Gansevoort Street. 1950–51. Oil, 30 x 40″
above de Kooning. Mailbox. 1948. Oil, enamel, and charcoal, 23¼ x 30″

below Baziotes. Jungle. 1951. Oil, 50 x 60⅛″
opposite Rothko. White and Greens in Blue. 1957. Oil, 8′6″ x 6′10″

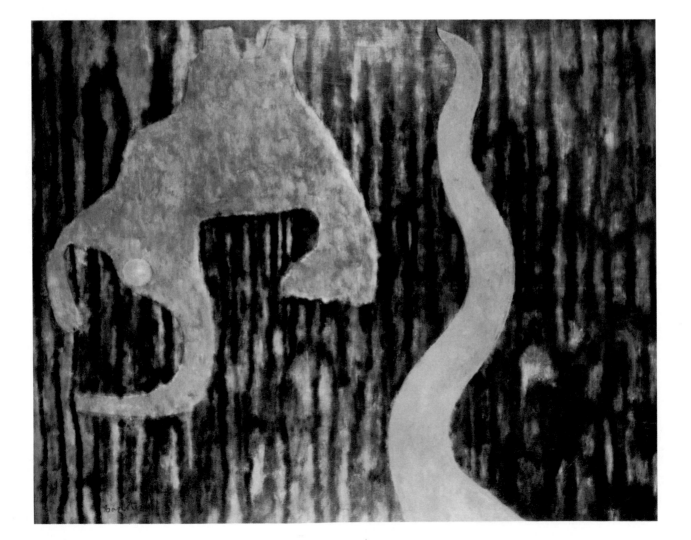

left Lipton. The Cloak. 1952. Bronze over steel, 8′ high
opposite Kiesler. Galaxy. 1951. Wood construction, 12′ high

above David Smith. The Banquet. 1951. Steel, 53″ x 6′8¾″
opposite David Smith. Voltri VI. 1962. Steel, 8′7″ x 8′6¾″

above Hague. Annandale-on-Hudson. 1962–63. Walnut, 49½″ high
opposite Ferber. Calligraph KC. 1963–64. Copper, 10′3″ high

below Lassaw. Galaxy of Andromeda. 1951. Lead over copper, 36⅜″ high
opposite Tomlin. Number 5. 1949. Oil, 69⅞ x 37⅞″

opposite above Brooks. Jackson. 1956. Oil, 66¾ x 69¾″
opposite below Guston. To Fellini. 1958. Oil, 69″ x 6′2″
above Kline. Corinthian, II. 1961. Oil, 6′7¾″ x 8′11″

above Hartigan. Salome. 1963. Oil, 6′6″ x 8′9½″
opposite Johns. 0 through 9. 1960. Oil, 6′ x 54″

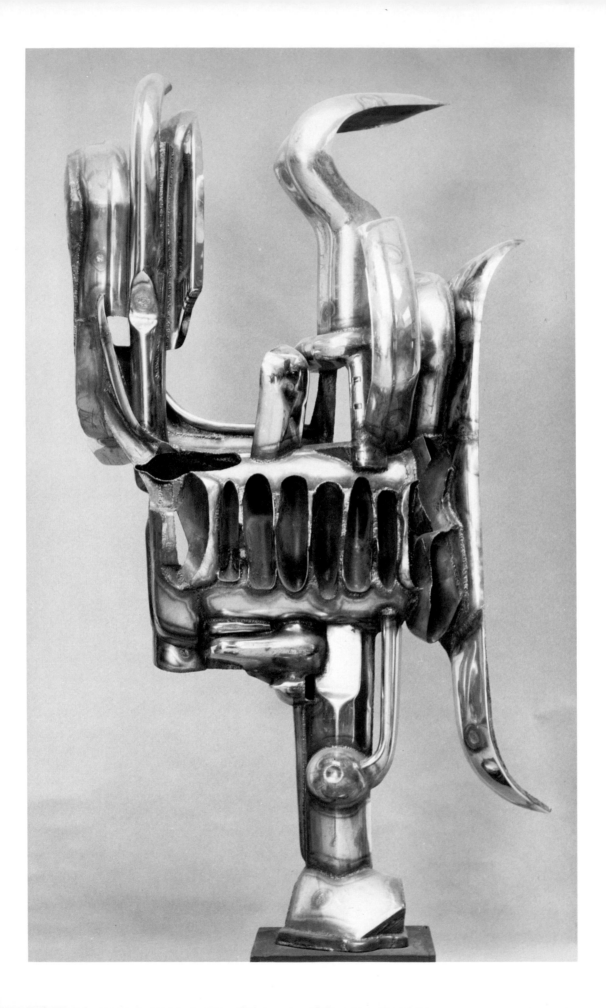

opposite Seley. Magister Ludi. 1962. Chromium-plated steel, 7′ x 45½ ″
above Bontecou. Untitled. 1960. Welded metal, canvas, and wire, 55 x 58″

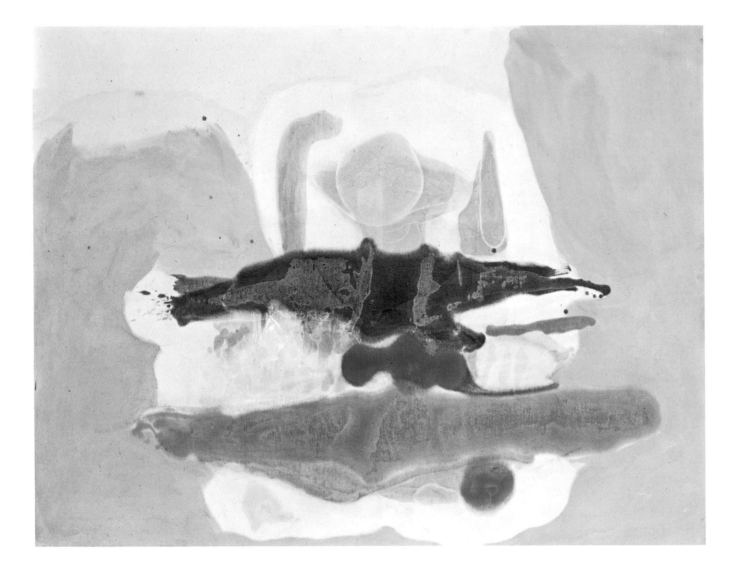

above Frankenthaler. Yellow Clearing. 1963. Oil, 53½ x 69½″
opposite Louis. Floral. 1959. Synthetic polymer paint, 8′5″ x 11′10″

above Nevelson. Atmosphere and Environment, VI. 1967. Enameled aluminum, 8' x 8'6"

opposite . Noguchi. Black Sun. 1960–63. Granite, 30" diameter

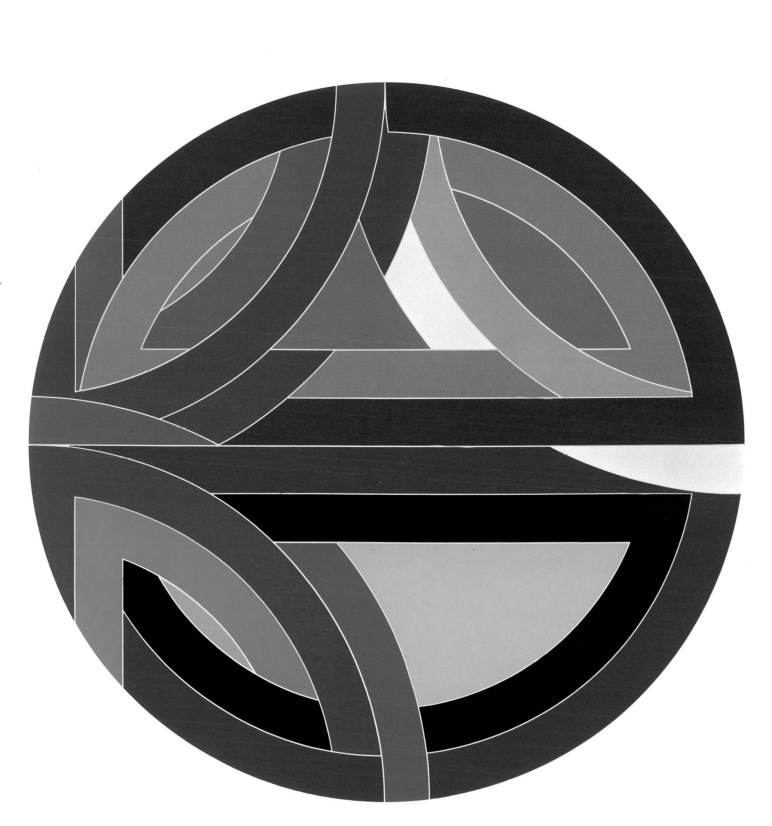

opposite Kelly. Green, Red. 1965. Oil, 7'6¼" x 7'6⅜"
above Frank Stella. Sinjerli Variation, III. 1968. Synthetic polymer paint, 10'2½" diameter

below Trova. Study: Falling Man (Car Man). 1966–67. Bronze, 20″ x 6′5⅞″
opposite Snelson. Fair Leda. 1968. Steel, 12′8½″ x 18′5″ x 10′10½″

opposite Arnaldo Pomodoro. Traveler's Column. 1965–66. Bronze, 11'10" high.
In background: Max Bill. Triangular Surface in Space. 1962.
below Meadmore. U Turn. 1968. Steel, 7'3" x 14' x 11'

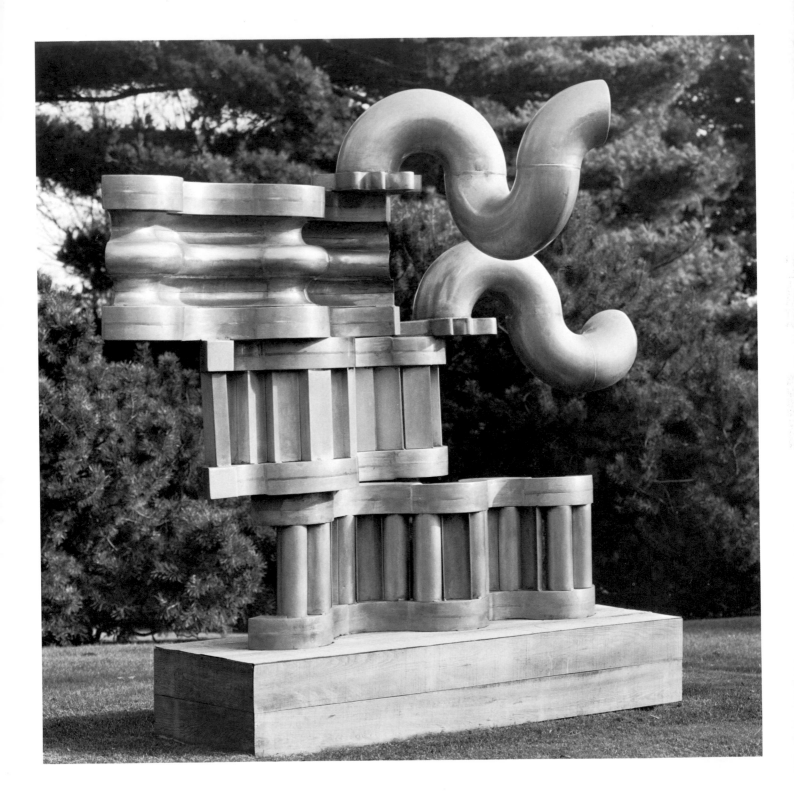

above Paolozzi. Akapotic Rose. 1965. Aluminum, 6′2½″ high
opposite Tajiri. Granny's Knot. 1967–68. Polyester resin and fiberglass, 11′6″ high

preceding pages Tony Smith. Wandering Rocks. 1967. Stainless steel. Largest piece, 22½ ″ x 8′2″ x 31″

CATALOGUE OF THE EXHIBITION
Twentieth-Century Art from the Nelson Aldrich Rockefeller Collection
May 26 through September 1, 1969
Directed by Dorothy C. Miller

129

Grateful acknowledgment is made to Carol Kinzel Uht for her patient and unfailing help in organizing the exhibition.

An asterisk preceding the title indicates that the work is illustrated. Unless enclosed in parentheses, dates appear on the works themselves or on stretchers or mats. Height precedes width; a third dimension, depth, is given for some sculptures. For prints, composition size is given. For illustrated books, page size is given; the largest dimension is used if the sheets vary. The term "sight" refers to approximate measurements taken without removal of a frame or mat from a work.   —D.C.M.

PAINTINGS, SCULPTURE, AND DRAWINGS

Appel, Karel. Dutch, born 1921. Lives in Paris.
Bird Woman. 1951. Oil on canvas, 57¼ x 38⅛″

Archipenko, Alexander. American, born Ukraine. 1887–1964. Worked in Paris 1908–21; to U.S.A. 1923.
*Standing Woman. (1923, possibly after a terra cotta of ca. 1920). Mahogany, 17½″ high. Illustrated p. 58

Armitage, Kenneth. British, born 1916.
People in a Wind. (1951). Bronze, 25½″ high

Arp, Jean. French, born Alsace. 1887–1966.
*Man with a Moustache. (ca. 1924). Oil on cardboard with cutouts, 21⅝ x 19½″. Illustrated p. 24
*Shell Crystal. (1938). Granite, 13 x 14¾″. Illustrated p. 69
Dream Animal. (1947). Bronze, 15½ x 10 x 7″
*Snake Movement. II. (1955). Concrete, 16¼″ x 28 x 23¼″. Illustrated p. 69
*Amphora of the Muse. (1959). Marble, 44¾″ high. Illustrated p.68

Balla, Giacomo. Italian, 1871–1958.
Flight of Swifts. 1913. Gouache on paper, 19⅝ x 29″ (sight)

Barlach, Ernst. German, 1870–1938.
The Skeptic. (1937). Bronze, 19¾ x 10⅝ x 7⅜″

Baziotes, William. American, 1912–1963.
*Jungle. 1951. Oil on canvas, 50 x 60⅛″. Illustrated p. 98

Beckmann, Max. German, 1884–1950. Worked in Amsterdam 1936–47; in U.S.A. 1947–50.
*Woman with a Parrot. 1946. Oil on canvas, 37¼ x 23¾″. Illustrated p. 90

Bell, Larry. American, born 1939.
Untitled (14-C). (1966–67). Tinted glass with chrome mounting, 14¼″ cube, on plexiglass pedestal, 43″ high

Blume, Peter. American, born Russia 1906. To U.S.A. 1911.
*Excavation. 1945. Oil on canvas, 21⅛ x 27″. Illustrated p. 92

Boccioni, Umberto. Italian, 1882–1916.
*States of Mind: The Farewells. (1911). Oil on canvas, 27¾ x 37⅞″. Illustrated p. 53

*States of Mind: Those Who Go. (1911). Oil on canvas, 27⅞ x 37¾″. Illustrated p. 52
*States of Mind: Those Who Stay. (1911). Oil on canvas, 27⅞ x 37¾″. Illustrated p. 52

Bontecou, Lee. American, born 1931.
*Untitled. (1960). Relief construction of welded metal, canvas, and wire, 55 x 58 x 15″. Illustrated p. 113

Brancusi, Constantin. French, born Rumania. 1876–1957. To Paris 1904.
*Bird in Space. (1926?). White marble, 6′2⅜″ high. Illustrated p. 61

Braque, Georges. French, 1882–1963.
Parc des Carrières, St. Denis. (1909–10). Oil on canvas, 16 x 17⅞″
*Clarinet. (1913). Pasted papers, charcoal, chalk, and oil on canvas, 37½ x 47⅜″. Illustrated p. 49
*Guitar, Newspaper, and Bottle. (1913–14). Oil on canvas, 28⅞ x 21¼″. Illustrated p. 50
*The Table. 1930. Oil and sand on canvas, 57⅝ x 30⅜″. Illustrated p. 59

Brooks, James. American, born 1906.
*Jackson. 1956. Oil on canvas, 66¾ x 69¾″. Illustrated p. 108

Bury, Pol. Belgian, born 1922.
Twenty-nine Balls on Two Slanting Planes. 1967. Construction of copper, with motor, 14⅛ x 13⅞ x 12″

Butler, Reg (Reginald Cotterell Butler). British, born 1913.
*Oracle. (1952; this cast 1956). Cast shell bronze welded to forged bronze armature, 33½″ x 6′1″ x 35½″. Illustrated p. 87
Girl with a Vest. (1953–54). Cast shell bronze, 68⅜″ high
*Manipulator. (1954). Cast shell bronze, 67 x 23¼ x 15″. Illustrated p. 88

Calder, Alexander. American, born 1898.
*The Golfer (John D. Rockefeller, Sr.). (ca. 1928). Wire construction, 15¼ x 9 x 12½″. Illustrated p. 32
*Spiny. (1942). Stabile: painted sheet aluminum, 26 x 30″. Illustrated p. 82
Black Rocker, Yellow Moon. (1949). Mobile-stabile: painted steel and wire, 23½ x 17⅜ x ca. 17″
*Flying Boomerangs. (1961). Mobile: painted sheet steel and steel wire, ca. 21″ x 9′8″. Illustrated p. 82
*Large Spiny. (1966, after the stabile of 1942). Stabile: painted sheet steel, 12′6″ x 17′6″ x 8′6″. Illustrated p. 83

Callery, Mary. American, born 1903. Lives in Paris.
Composition, XIV (Letter C). (1960). Steel and brass, 6½ x 10¼ x 12″

Castellanos, Julio. Mexican, 1905–1947.
*St. John's Day. (1938). Oil on canvas, 15¾ x 18⅞″. Illustrated p. 92

Chadwick, Lynn. British, born 1914.

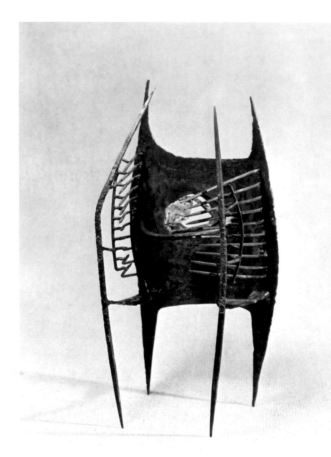

Chadwick. Inner Eye. 1952

Barley Fork. (1952). Wrought iron, 20⅞″ high, 26½″ at fullest arc

*Inner Eye. (1952). Wrought iron with cullet, 15⅜ x 17½″. Illustrated p. 130

de Chirico, Giorgio. Italian, born Greece 1888.

*The Song of Love. (1914). Oil on canvas, 28⅜ x 23½″. Illustrated p. 10

Dechar, Peter. American, born 1942.

Pear 68-11. 1968. Oil on canvas, 52″ x 6′

Delvaux, Paul. Belgian, born 1897.

*The Watchman, II. 1961. Oil on composition board, 48″ x 8′. Illustrated p. 93

The Mirage. 1967. Watercolor and ink on paper, 24⅜ x 39⅛″

Demuth, Charles. American, 1883–1935.

Tulips. 1929. Watercolor on paper, 17⅛ x 11¾″ (sight)

van Dongen, Kees (Cornelis T. M. van Dongen). Dutch, 1877–1968. Lived in Paris.

*Woman in a Large Hat. (1908). Oil on canvas, 39½ x 32″. Illustrated p. 44

Duchamp-Villon, Raymond. French, 1876–1918.

*The Horse (Le Cheval majeur). 1914 (cast 3 of second enlarged version, 1966). Bronze, 59 x 35½ x 53½″. Illustrated p. 54

Eielson, Jorge. Peruvian, born 1924. Lives in Rome.

*Red Quipu. (1964). Tempera and knotted cloth on canvas, 42¾ x 39⅝″. Illustrated p. 27

Evans, Merlyn. British, born 1910.

Composition, II. 1962–63. Oil on canvas, 56″ x 6′6¾″

Feeley, Paul. American, 1913–1966.

Etamin. 1965. Synthetic polymer paint on canvas, 59⅞ x 59⅞″

Feininger, Lyonel. American, 1871–1956. In Germany 1887–1936; to U.S.A. 1937.

The Burglar. (1903). Pen and ink and gouache on paper, 5½ x 8⅝″

Big Cloud, III. 1948. Pen and ink, watercolor, and wash on paper, 11¾ x 18½″ (sight)

Ship in a Storm. 1953. Pen and ink, watercolor, and wash on paper, 12 x 18½″

Ferber, Herbert. American, born 1906.

*Calligraph KC. (1963–64). Welded copper, 10′3″ x 68″ x 40½″. Illustrated p. 105

Frankenthaler, Helen. American, born 1928.

*Yellow Clearing. (1963). Oil on canvas, 53½ x 69½″. Illustrated p. 114

Three Color Space. (1966). Synthetic polymer paint on canvas, 7′8⅝″ x 7′10″

Gabo, Naum. American, born Russia 1890. Worked in Germany, Paris, England; to U.S.A. 1947.

*Construction in Space, X. (1952–53). Construction of plexiglass and nylon wire, with aluminum base, 28″ high. Illustrated p. 67

Giacometti, Alberto. Swiss, 1901–1966. Lived in Paris.

*Spoon Woman. (1926). Bronze, 57″ high. Illustrated p. 84

*Woman with Her Throat Cut. 1932 (this cast 1950). Bronze, 8 x 34½ x 25″. Illustrated p. 85

Nude. 1932–36 (this cast 1960). Bronze, 58 x 10⅜″

*City Square. (1948). Bronze, 8½ x 25⅜ x 17¼″. Illustrated p.86

Walking Quickly under the Rain. (1949). Bronze, 17⅝ x 32 x 6″

Glarner, Fritz. American, born Switzerland 1899. To U.S.A. 1936.

*Relational Painting, Tondo 36. (1954–55). Oil on composition board, 41″ diameter. Illustrated p. 131

Gleizes, Albert. French, 1881–1953.

Football Players. 1912–13. Oil on canvas, 7′5″ x 6′

Gonzalez, Julio. Spanish, 1876–1942. Worked in Paris from 1900.

*Reclining Figure. (1934). Wrought iron, 17¾ x 37″. Illustrated p. 66

Gottlieb, Adolph. American, born 1903.

*Transfiguration. 1958. Oil on canvas, 7′6″ x 60″. Illustrated p. 94

Gris, Juan. Spanish, 1887–1927. Worked in Paris.

*Guitar, Bottle, and Glass. (1914). Pasted papers, gouache, and crayon on canvas, 36⅛ x 25½″. Illustrated p. 51

*The Sideboard. 1917. Oil on plywood, 46⅞ x 28¾″. Illustrated p. 55

Guston, Philip. American, born 1913.

*To Fellini. (1958). Oil on canvas, 69″ x 6′2″. Illustrated p. 108

Hague, Raoul. American, born Constantinople 1905. To U.S.A. 1921.

*Annandale-on-Hudson. (1962–63). Walnut, 49½ x 32 x 27½″. Illustrated p. 104

Hartigan, Grace. American, born 1922.

*Salome. 1963. Oil on canvas, 6′6″ x 8′9½″. Illustrated p. 110

Higgins, Edward. American, born 1930.

Dinghy. (1960). Welded steel and plaster, 26¾ x 41⅞ x 6¾″

Hinman, Charles B. American, born 1932.

Number 3. (1965). Synthetic polymer paint on shaped canvas over wood framework, 60″ x 7′ x 16″

Ipousteguy, Jean. French, born 1920.

*Alexander before Ecbatane. (1965). Bronze, 68″ x ca. 12′ x 39⅜″. Illustrated p. 89

Jawlensky, Alexey. Russian, 1864–1941. Worked in Germany and Switzerland.

*Cottage in the Woods. 1903. Oil on wood, 20¼ x 19¼″. Illustrated p. 19

*The Spanish Girl. (1912). Oil on paper, mounted on cardboard, 27 x 19¼″. Illustrated p. 43

Johns, Jasper. American, born 1930.

0–9. (1958–59). Encaustic on newspaper on canvas, 20⅛ x 35″

*0 through 9. 1960. Oil on canvas, 6′ x 54″. Illustrated p. 111

Glarner. Relational Painting, Tondo 36. 1954–55

Kalinowski. The Eye of Horus. 1964

Kalinowski, Horst-Egon. German, born 1924. Lives in Paris.
*The Eye of Horus. 1964. Leather over wood construction, 30 x
21⅞ x 9″. Illustrated p. 132

Kandinsky, Wassily. Russian, 1866–1944. Worked in Germany
and France.
*Autumn Landscape, Murnau. 1908. Oil on composition board,
27¼ x 37¼″ (sight). Illustrated p. 42

Kelly, Ellsworth. American, born 1923.
*Green, Red. (1965). Oil on canvas, 7′6¼″ x 7′6⅜″. Illustrated
p. 118

Kiesler, Frederick. American, born Vienna. 1890–1965. To U.S.A.
1926.
*Galaxy. (1951). Wood construction, 12′ high, dimensions around
base 13′ x 11′6″ x 10′10″ x 7′. Illustrated p. 101

Kikuhata, Mokuma. Japanese, born 1935.
Roulette: Chance. (1964). Enamel paint and assemblage of metal
objects on wood, 42¼ x 25½ x 4½″

Klee, Paul. German, 1879–1940. Born and died in Switzerland.
Yellow Harbor. 1921. Pen and ink, transfer process, watercolor,
and wash on paper, 12½ x 19″
*Sharp Profile. 1924. Pen and ink, transfer process, and wash on
paper, 10 x 11¼″. Illustrated p. 25
*The Jester. 1927. Oil on cardboard, 28½ x 18¾″. Illustrated
p. 25
The Wall, I. 1929. Watercolor and wash on paper, 18 x 10¼″
Prince. 1930. Pen and ink and watercolor on pink paper, 18¾
x 12½″
*Fear. 1934. Oil on burlap, 19¾ x 21¼″. Illustrated p. 76
*Heroic Strokes of the Bow (Heroische Bogenstriche). 1938.
Tempera on paper on cloth with gesso backing, 28¾ x 20⅞″.
Illustrated p. 77

Kline, Franz. American, 1910–1962.
*Corinthian, II. (1961). Oil on canvas, 6′7¾″ x 8′11″. Illustrated
p. 109

Kolbe, Georg. German, 1877–1947.
Grief. (1921). Bronze, 15¾ x 22″

de Kooning, Willem. American, born The Netherlands 1904. To
U.S.A. 1926.
*Mailbox. (1948). Oil, enamel, and charcoal on paper, 23¼ x
30″. Illustrated p. 97
*Gansevoort Street. (1950–51). Oil on cardboard, mounted on
composition board, 30 x 40″. Illustrated p. 96

Lachaise, Gaston. American, born France. 1882–1935. To U.S.A.
1906.
*Standing Woman. 1927 (1912–27; this cast 1967). Bronze,
70½″ high. Note: This work has also been called Elevation. Illustrated p. 71
*Torso. (1932). Bronze, 7⅝″ high. Illustrated p. 72

Lam, Wifredo. Cuban, born 1902. Worked in Paris; lives in Italy.

*Chemical Nuptials. (1944). Oil and charcoal on canvas, 61¾ x 49¾". Illustrated p. 26

Lassaw, Ibram. American, born Egypt 1913. To U.S.A. 1921.

*Galaxy of Andromeda. (1951). Lead over copper, welded, 36⅜ x 39¼ x 20⅝". Illustrated p. 106

Léger, Fernand. French, 1881–1955.

*Armistice. 1918. Oil on canvas, 21¾ x 15". Illustrated p. 56

*Woman with a Book. 1923. Oil on canvas, 45½ x 32". Illustrated p. 57

Lehmbruck, Wilhelm. German, 1881–1919.

*Torso. (1910). Cast stone, 45" high. Illustrated p. 45

*Dancer. (1913–14). Cast stone, 11½" high. Illustrated p. 45

Liberman, Alexander. American, born Ukraine 1912. To U.S.A. 1941.

Omicron, III. 1961. Oil on canvas, mounted on composition board, 6'8" diameter

Lichtenstein, Roy. American, born 1923.

Modern Painting with Zigzag. 1967. Oil and synthetic polymer paint on canvas, 68" x 6'10⅛"

Lipchitz, Jacques. American, born Lithuania 1891. In France 1909–41; to U.S.A. 1941.

*Seated Man with Guitar. 1922. Granite, 15⅞" high. Illustrated p. 58

Lipton, Seymour. American, born 1903.

*The Cloak. (1952). Bronze over steel, 8' high. Illustrated p. 100

Storm Bird. (1953). Nickel silver over steel, 20 x 37 x 9⅝"

Louis, Morris. American, 1912–1962.

*Floral. 1959. Synthetic polymer paint on canvas, 8'5" x 11'10". Illustrated p. 115

Maillol, Aristide. French, 1861–1944.

*Night. (1902–09; this cast after 1944). Bronze, 41½ x 40⅝ x 24". Illustrated p. 37

Chained Action: Torso of the Monument to Louis-Auguste Blanqui. (1906). Bronze, 47" high

*Bather Putting Up Her Hair. (1930, after a small figure of 1898). Bronze, 61½" high. Illustrated p. 36

Mallary, Robert. American, born 1917.

Head of a Bull. (1958). Composition stone in resin base, 33 x 33"

Matisse, Henri. French, 1869–1954.

*Reclining Nude, I. (1907). Bronze, 13½" x 19¾". Illustrated p. 40

*Collioure. (1911). Oil on canvas, 24¾ x 20⅜". Illustrated p. 38

*Italian Woman. (1915). Oil on canvas, 45¾ x 35¼". Illustrated p. 39

Head of a Girl. (ca. 1918). Pencil, 14 x 9" (sight)

*Seated Nude. (1925). Bronze, 31½ x 29⅝". Illustrated p. 40

*Nude in the Studio. 1935. Pen and ink on paper, 17¾ x 22⅜". Illustrated p. 21

Nagare. Jubilee. 1965

Window at Tahiti. 1935. Tapestry after a cartoon by Matisse commissioned by Mme Marie Cuttoli. Beauvais low warp, silk and wool, 7′4″ x 68″

Meadmore, Clement. American, born Australia 1929. To U.S.A. 1963.

*U Turn. (1968). Cor-ten steel, painted, 7′3″ x 14′ x 11′. Illustrated p. 123

Miró, Joan. Spanish, born 1893. Worked in Paris from 1920.

*Collage. (1933). Pasted papers, charcoal, pencil, and ink on sandpaper, mounted on canvas, 42¾ x 28⅛″. Illustrated p. 80

*Painting. 1933. Oil on canvas, 51¼ x 6′5″. Illustrated p. 79

*L'Hirondelle d'amour. (1934). Oil on canvas, 6′6½″ x 8′1½″. Illustrated p. 81

Seated Woman. 1935. Oil on cardboard, mounted on canvas, 29⅝ x 41⅝″

Modigliani, Amedeo. Italian, 1884–1920. Worked in France.

*The Dreamer. (1918). Oil on canvas, 23½ x 36¼″. Illustrated p. 41

Mondrian, Piet. Dutch, 1872–1944. Worked in Paris 1912–14, 1919–38; in New York 1940–44.

*Large Composition A. (1919). Oil on canvas, 35½ x 35¾″. Illustrated p. 60

Moore, Henry. British, born 1898.

Reclining Figure, I. (1945). Bronze, 15″ long

*Family Group. (1948–49; this cast 1951). Bronze, 59¼ x 46½″. Illustrated p. 73.

*King and Queen. (1952). Bronze, 10¾ x 8¼″. Illustrated p. 72

*Knife Edge Two Piece. (1962; large version 1965–66). Bronze, 9 x 12′. Illustrated p. 75

*Nuclear Energy. (1964). Bronze, 45½ x 28 x 27″. Illustrated p. 74

Morandi, Giorgio. Italian, 1890–1964.

*Still Life. 1939. Oil on canvas, 17⅛ x 20¾″. Illustrated p. 91

Motherwell, Robert. American, born 1915.

*Granada: Elegy to the Spanish Republic, II. (1949). Oil on paper, mounted on composition board, 48 x 56⅛″. Illustrated p. 95

Beside the Sea, VIII. 1962. Oil on paper, 28⅞ x 22⅞″

Beside the Sea, XII. 1962. Oil on paper, 28¾ x 22¾″

Nadelman, Elie. American, born Poland. 1882–1946. Worked in Paris 1903–14; to U.S.A. 1914.

*Standing Bull. (1915). Bronze, 6⅝ x 11¼″. Illustrated p. 32

*Circus Woman, I. (ca. 1924; this cast 1965). Bronze, 49¼″ high. Illustrated p. 70

*Circus Woman, II. (ca. 1924; this cast 1965). Bronze, 44¾″ high. Illustrated p. 70

Two Circus Women. (ca. 1930; this cast 1951). Bronze, 61¼″ high

Two Nudes (ca. 1931; this cast 1949). Bronze, 59″ high

Nagare, Masayuki. Japanese, born 1923.

*Jubilee. 1965. Black granite, 28½ x 11½ x 17½″. Illustrated p. 133

Negret, Edgar. Colombian, born 1920. Lives in Paris.

*Magical Apparatus, II. (1954). Painted iron, 26½″ high. Illustrated p. 27

Nevelson, Louise. American, born Ukraine 1900. To U.S.A. 1903.

*White Column from "Dawn's Wedding Feast." (1959). Painted wood construction in two sections, 46¼ x 13½ x 11″ and 46½ x 14 x 12⅜″. Illustrated p. 31

*Atmosphere and Environment, VI. (1967). Enameled aluminum construction, 8′ x 8′6″ x 48″. Illustrated p. 116

Transparent Sculpture, VII. (1967–68). Plexiglass construction, 20¾ x 10⅞ x 7⅛″

Noguchi, Isamu. American, born 1904.

Celebration. (1952). Cast iron, 17⅞ x 21 x 1⅜″

Small Child. (1952). Ceramic (Karatzu), 6¼ x 6¼″

*Mr. One-Man. (1952). Ceramic (Kasama). 11¼ x 9⅞ x 8½″. Illustrated p. 33

*Black Sun. (1960–63). Black Tamba granite, 30″ diameter. Illustrated p. 117

Paolozzi, Eduardo. British, born 1924.

*Akapotic Rose. (1965). Cast and welded aluminum, 6′2½″ x 9′3″ x 50″. Illustrated p. 124

Picasso, Pablo. Spanish, born 1881. In France since 1904.

*Study for "The Actor" with Profiles of Fernande. (1904–05). Pencil on paper, 18½ x 12⅜″ (sight). Illustrated p. 17

Boy on Horseback. (1906). Pen and ink on paper, 16 x 12¾″

Kneeling Woman Combing Her Hair. (1906). Bronze, 16⅝″ high

*Harvesters. (1907). Oil on canvas, 25½ x 32″. Illustrated p. 46

Kneeling Woman. (1908). Charcoal on paper, 24⅜ x 18½″. Note: Study for the painting Three Women, 1908

*Girl with a Mandolin (Fanny Tellier). 1910. Oil on canvas, 39½ x 29″. Illustrated p. 47

Woman with a Mandolin. (1910). Oil on canvas, oval, 31½ x 25¼″

*Still Life: Le Torero. (1911). Oil on canvas, 18¼ x 15⅛″. Illustrated p. 48

*Guitar. (1913). Pasted papers and charcoal on blue paper, 24⅜ x 18⅛″ (sight). Frontispiece

*Still Life: "Job." 1916. Oil on canvas, 17 x 13¾″. Illustrated p. 48

Figure Study, Back. (1920–21). Charcoal on gray paper, 24¾ x 18¾″

Study of a Hand. 1921. Pastel on paper, 8¼ x 12⅝″

Woman's Head. (1926). Charcoal and chalk on paper, 25 x 19″

*Pitcher and Bowl of Fruit. 1931. Oil on canvas, 51½ x 64″. Illustrated p. 62

*Two Women. 1934. Tapestry after a cartoon by Picasso commissioned by Mme Marie Cuttoli. Beauvais low warp, silk and wool, 6′2⅜″ x 68″. Note: This tapestry has also been called Oedipus and the Sphinx. Illustrated p. 22

*Interior with a Girl Drawing. 1935. Oil on canvas, 51⅛″ x 6′4⅝″. Illustrated p. 63

*The Striped Bodice. 1943. Oil on canvas, 39⅜ x 32⅛". Illustrated p. 64

Condor. (1949). Painted ceramic, 13 x 13½"

*Red and White Owl. 1953. Painted ceramic, 13¾" high. Illustrated p. 33

The Woman and the Dwarf. 1953. Brush and ink on paper, 13¾ x 10⅜"

Models Posing. 1954. Brush and ink on paper, 9⅜ x 12½"

The Studio Visit, IV. 1954. Brush and ink on paper, 9½ x 12⅝"

The Studio Visit, VI. 1954. Brush and ink on paper, 9⅜ x 12⅝"

The Models. 1954. Brush and ink on paper, 9½ x 12⅝"

Woman Painter and Model. 1954. Brush and ink on paper, 9⅜ x 12½"

Sylvette, Red Background. 1954. Oil on canvas, 32 x 25½"

*The Bathers. (1956). Bronze, after wood. Six figures: Bather, 8'8" x 33⅜"; Man with joined hands, 8'¾" x 32½"; Fountain man, 7'¼" x 25⅝"; Diver, 6'6½" x 69"; Bather, 69¾ x 19½"; Head, 53½ x 27". Illustrated p. 65

Man with a Lamb and People. 1967. Colored crayons on paper, 19¼ x 23¾" (sight)

Pistoletto, Michelangelo. Italian, born 1933.

Green Curtains. (1967). Oil on paper, pasted on stainless steel, 47¼ x 59"

Polesello, Rogelio. Argentine, born 1939.

Black. 1966. Synthetic polymer paint on canvas, 41¼ x 33⅜"

Pomodoro, Arnaldo. Italian, born 1926.

*Traveler's Column. 1965–66. Bronze, 11'10" high, 19¾" diameter. Illustrated p. 122

Rodriguez-Larrain y Balta, Emilio. Peruvian, born 1928. Lives in Paris.

Mantilla and Carnations, XIII. (1961). Mixed media on paper, mounted on wood, 39 x 39"

Rothko, Mark. American, born Latvia 1903. To U.S.A. 1913.

*White and Greens in Blue. (1957). Oil on canvas, 8'6" x 6'10". Illustrated p. 99

Rouault, Georges. French, 1871–1958.

*The Judge. 1930. Ink, wash, and pastel on paper, 22¾ x 16¾". Illustrated p. 19

Schmidt, Julius. American, born 1923.

Iron Sculpture. (1960). Cast iron, 16¾" high

Schwitters, Kurt. British, born Germany. 1887–1948. In England 1940–48.

*Merz 212: "Detektiv-K. . . ." 1921. Pasted papers, 7⅛ x 5⅝". Illustrated p. 78

Merz 319: Green Spot (Grünfleck). 1921. Pasted papers and cloth with paint, 5⅛ x 4⅛"

Merz 430: "Feine 100 gr." 1922. Pasted papers and ribbon, 8½ x 6¾" (sight)

White Circle (Weisser Kreis). (1922). Pasted papers with paint, 6 x 4⅝"

Stankiewicz. Untitled XXXII. 1960

*"Vollmilch." 1928. Pasted papers, 5⅜ x 4⅛". Illustrated p. 78

"...land." 1946. Pasted papers and pencil, 9½ x 7½" (sight)

"...perial." 1946. Pasted papers, 11¾ x 9⅝" (sight)

Segal, George. American, born 1924.

Shower Curtain. (1966). Plaster, 70 x 50 x 19½"

Seley, Jason. American, born 1919.

*Magister Ludi. (1962). Welded chromium-plated steel automobile bumpers, 7' x 45½". Illustrated p. 112

Smith, David. American, 1906–1965.

*The Banquet. 1951. Painted steel, 53" x 6'8¾". Illustrated p. 102

*Voltri VI. 1962. Steel, 8'7" x 8'6¾" x 25½". Illustrated p. 103

Smith, Tony. American, born 1912.

*Wandering Rocks. (1967). Stainless steel, vapor-blasted. Five pieces: Dud, 22½" x 8'2" x 31"; Slide, 22½" x 6'4" x 27½"; Crocus, 47 x 45 x 27"; Shaft, 6' x 45" x 27½"; Smohawk, 27½ x 47 x 22½". Illustrated pp. 126–127

Snelson, Kenneth. American, born 1927.

*Fair Leda. 1968. Stainless steel tubes and cable, 12'8½" x 18'5" x 10'10½". Illustrated p. 121

Somaini, Francesco. Italian, born 1926.

Wounded, III. (1960). Cast iron, 13 x 17¼ x 14"

Stahly, François. French, born Germany 1911.

Brown and Black, V. 1966. Wall hanging designed by François Stahly and executed by Claude Stahly: appliquéd cotton, linen, and wool, 9'3½" x 10'

Stankiewicz, Richard. American, born 1922.

*Untitled XXXII. 1960. Welded scrap metal, 37 x 36 x 33". Illustrated p. 135

Stella, Frank. American, born 1936.

Avicenna. (1960). Aluminum paint on canvas, 6 x 6'

*Sinjerli Variation, III. 1968. Fluorescent synthetic polymer paint on canvas, 10'2½" diameter. Illustrated p. 119

Tajiri, Shinkichi G. American, born 1923. Lives in the Netherlands.

*Granny's Knot. (1967-68). Polyester resin and fiberglass, 11'6" high. Illustrated p. 125

Tobey, Mark. American, born 1890. Lives in Basel.

Jazz Singer. 1954. Gouache on paper, 16⅝ x 9⅜" (sight)

*Voyagers, III. 1954. Tempera on paper, 17¾ x 11⅜" (sight). Illustrated p. 28

Tomlin, Bradley Walker. American, 1899–1953.

*Number 5. (1949). Oil on canvas, 69⅞ x 37⅞". Illustrated p. 107

Trova, Ernest. American, born 1927.

*Study: Falling Man (Car Man). (1966-67). Bronze, 20" x 6'5⅞" x 30⅞". Illustrated p. 120

Uecker, Günther. German, born 1930.

Heart. 1964. Nails projecting from canvas-covered board, painted, 34¼" diameter

PRINTS AND ILLUSTRATED BOOKS

Bontecou, Lee. American, born 1931.

Fifth Stone, Sixth Stone. By Tony Towle. West Islip, New York: Universal Limited Art Editions, 1968. 6 etching and aquatints, and 1 etching on cloth binding. 20 x 13"

Braque, Georges. French, 1882–1963.

Braque le patron. By Jean Paulhan. Paris: Fernand Mourlot, 1945. 1 lithograph, 14⅜ x 11⅛". Jacques Anthoine-Legrain binding

L'Ordre des oiseaux. By Saint-John Perse. Arles, 1962. 9 full-page and 3 vignette etchings, 21¼ x 16½"

Chagall, Marc. French, born Russia 1887.

Fables. By Jean de la Fontaine. Paris: Tériade, 1952. 100 etchings in two volumes, 15 x 11". Watercolor, pen and ink drawing on first flyleaf

Frasconi, Antonio. Uruguayan, born 1919. In U.S.A. since 1945.

The Fulton Fish Market. (New York, 1953). 12 woodcuts, 20 x 13⅛"

Glarner, Fritz. American, born Switzerland 1899. To U.S.A. 1936.

Recollection. By Fritz Glarner. West Islip, New York: Universal Limited Art Editions, 1968. 15 lithographs, 14¾ x 11⅜"

Matisse, Henri. French, 1869–1954.

*Odalisque in Striped Pantaloons. (1925). Lithograph, 21½ x 17⅜". Illustrated p. 21

Poésies. By Stéphane Mallarmé. Lausanne: Albert Skira. 1932. 29 etchings, 13 x 10". Added suite of 29 etchings with notations

Miró, Joan. Spanish, born 1893. Worked in Paris.

A toute epreuve. By Paul Eluard. Geneva: Gérald Cramer, 1958. 79 woodcuts, some with collage, 12⅝ x 9¾". Reworked and embellished proof on flyleaf, and added suite of woodcuts on Japan paper

Picasso, Pablo. Spanish, born 1881. In France since 1904.

*Minotauromachy. (1935). Etching, 19½ x 27⅜". Illustrated p. 34

Toulouse-Lautrec, Henri de. French, 1864–1901.

The Englishman at the Moulin Rouge. (1892). Color lithograph, 20⅞ x 14¾"

Miss May Belfort Bowing. (1895). Lithograph, 14½ x 10"

Ride in the Country. (1897). Color lithograph, 14½ x 19"

Various artists

L'Estampe originale. Paris: Journal des Artistes, March 1893–December 1894, March 1895. Volumes I–VIII, X. 90 prints in various media, 24 x 16½". Among the artists represented: Bernard, Bonnard, Carrière, Gauguin, Pissarro, Redon, Renoir, Rodin, Toulouse-Lautrec, Vallotton, and Whistler

L'Epreuve. December 1894–1895. Volume I, 1–12. 120 prints in various media, 15 x 11". Among the artists represented: Bonnard Denis, Gauguin, Maillol, Vuillard

Oliver Baker: 29 bottom, 60, 78 bottom, 84; Ferdinand Boesch: 116, 120; Brenwasser: 29 top; Rudolph Burckhardt: 48 bottom, 113; Byron Gallery: 123; Geoffrey Clements: 28, 42, 100, 108 bottom, 109; Colten: 67; Niki Ekstrom: 117; Leonard Hutton Galleries: 19, 44; Peter A. Juley & Son: 21 bottom; M. Knoedler & Co., Inc.: 54; Ugo Mulas: 103; Eric Pollitzer: 23 bottom, 80, 118 (courtesy Sidney Janis Gallery); Percy Rainford: 82 top, 92 bottom, 95, 98; Ben Rose: 101; John D. Schiff: 25 bottom, 72 bottom (courtesy The Eakins Press); Service de Documentation Photographique, Réunion des Musées Nationaux, Versailles: 65; Adolph Studly: 25 top, 40 bottom, 45 top, 58 left; Soichi Sunami: 17, 19 top, 21 top, 23 top, 32 top, 40 top, 47, 48 top, 51, 63, 69 bottom, 73, 77, 85, 86, 87, 92 top, 97, 130; Shinkichi Tajiri: 125; Charles Uht: cover, 15, 20 top, 20 bottom, 22, 24, 26, 27 top, 27 bottom, 30, 31, 32 bottom, 33 top, 33 bottom, 34, 36, 37, 41, 43, 45 bottom, 50, 52 top, 52 bottom, 53, 56, 58 right, 61, 64, 68, 69 top, 70 left, 70 right, 71, 72 top, 74, 75, 76, 78 top, 79, 82 bottom, 83, 88, 89, 90, 91, 93, 94, 102, 104, 105, 106, 107, 108 top, 110, 112, 121, 122, 124, 126–127, 132, 133, 135; Malcolm Varon: frontispiece, 10, 38, 39, 46, 49, 55, 57, 62, 81, 96, 99, 111, 114, 115, 119, 131.

INDEX

cover Calder. Large Spiny. 1966 (after stabile of 1942).
In background: Marino Marini. Horse. 1951. *Photograph by Charles Uht*